MY FAVORITE

PATTERNS

for Dressing Antique Dolls

1865–1925

MY FAVORITE PATTERNS
for
DRESSING ANTIQUE DOLLS

(1865 – 1925)

EVELYN ACKERMAN

Drawings and Photographs
by Evelyn Ackerman

Foreword by Edward Maeder
Curator of Costumes and Textiles
Los Angeles County Museum of Art

Revised Edition
with selections from and additions to twenty years of creating authentically styled patterns

Gold Horse Publishing

Two women from different generations have
had a profound influence on my life
my mother, Sarah
my daughter, Laura Beth

To them I dedicate this book

Book Design: Evelyn Ackerman

Frontispiece: Pattern G-10 modeled by a beautiful French H.

Inquiries should be addressed to: Gold Horse Publishing, P.O. Box 151, Annapolis, Maryland 21404

ISBN#0-912823-34-8.

"Walking Dress Pattern for a Late 1860s Fashion-type 12-1/2in (32cm) Doll" (*Doll Reader*, April 1988)
"A Trousseau for a Rohmer" (*Doll News*, Summer 1989)
"An Edwardian Outfit for a Six-Inch Lady" (*Dollmaking*, Fall 1989)
"A Flapper-Style, Fur-Trimmed Fall Suit" (*Dollmaking*, Winter 1989)
"Princess-Style Dress" (*Dollmaking*, Spring 1990)

In addition to new material, the following author copyrighted pattern portfolios are incorporated in part or in whole into this book:

Mais, Oui, It's French! (© 1970)
A Portfolio of Patterns for Early 20th Century Boy Dolls (© 1971)
A Portfolio of Patterns for Miniature Dolls (© 1972)
A Porfolio of Bonnet Patterns for Antique Dolls (© 1974)
A Potpourri of Patterns for Antique Dolls (© 1975)
French No. 2 Patterns (French Doll Dress Patterns) (© 1977)
A Portfolio of Patterns for Dollhouse Dolls (© 1977)
Pattern EA-7 (Schoenhut Boy's Suit) (© 1977)
La Haute Couturiere - Part I (© 1980)
La Haute Couturiere - Part II (© 1981)
La Haute Couturiere - Part III (© 1981)

CONTENTS

Late nineteenth century French dolls wear dresses made from the author's first group of authentically styled patterns.
(Photograph: Bob Lopez)

LIST OF
ILLUSTRATED DOLLS

The petite Bru stands alongside her Victorian trunk and wardrobe. She wears a two-piece dress made from Pattern No. F-18.

FOREWORD

Dress patterns have survived from as early as the first decades of the sixteenth century. A number of those rather careless guides, presumably used by a tailor, were found and exhibited in Linz, Austria, in 1970. The well known *Il Libro del Sarto* (Tailor's Book), from the 1570s in Venice, was published in facsimile in 1988. It contains no less than fourteen patterns for the costumes of men and women as well as church vestments.

The first published book of clothing patterns was printed in Spain in 1589. *Tailor's Pattern Book,* by Juan de Alcega, was printed in a facsimile edition with a complete English translation in 1979. Although primarily dedicated to men's fashion, there are a few women's garments. It was probably conceived as a tool to teach the recently invaded peoples of Central and South America how to dress in the "Spanish style." The imposition of a dress code was another method of transforming a native culture's dress into the forms preferred in Europe.

Tailors and dressmakers in the seventeenth and eighteenth centuries had access to published dress patterns, but it was not until the nineteenth century that full-scale dress patterns became available to the masses. Fashion journals, such as *Godey's Lady's Book,* had included scaled-down patterns since the 1830s, but with the arrival of *Harper's Bazar,* in 1868, full scale paper patterns were available to an international community.

Pattern drafting systems of varying complexity were marketed throughout the nineteenth century. Their history is the subject of an excellent book published by the Smithsonian Institution, in 1979, titled *Cutting a Fashionable Fit,* by Claudia B. Kidwell.

Although books such as *The History of Costume,* by Blanche Payne (1957), and *Costumes for the Stage,* by Lucy Barton (1960), contain a few patterns drawn to scale, it was not until 1964, when Janet Arnold published her first *Patterns of Fashion 1660-1860* that publication of patterns were the main preoccupation of an author. Two years later she followed this with another pattern book, *Patterns of Fashion 1860-1940.* These two volumes, as well as both *The Cut of Men's Clothes 1600-1900* (1964) by Norah Waugh, and *The Cut of Women's Clothes (1600-1900)* (1968), published after her death, have become indispensable to those involved in theater, historical reenactments and films.

Of course, most of these sources have not been entirely satisfactory for the creator of doll clothes. The current book by author Evelyn Ackerman is an answer to the many prayers which have gone for so long unheeded. The rich variety of historical periods, types of dolls and useful information will bring pleasure and satisfaction to everyone from the amateur to the specialist.

Edward Maeder
Curator, Costumes and Textiles

INTRODUCTION

When I was a child, I would watch my mother sew and I would feel a sense of great wonder, even awe, at her skill. Her ability was obvious even to my inexperienced eyes. With incredible speed she could whip up any garment—even the most complicated—in a matter of hours. All patterns were her own creation. These she would work out quickly on our breakfast-room table, using ordinary newspaper. Most other needlework skills were included in her repetoire. I still have in my possession a few of the articles she made, among them a beaded purse, an embroidered tablecloth and a crocheted shawl. The garments my mother made have long since disappeared, but, with possessive zeal, I have saved and cherished inconsequential items that belonged to her, such as fabric, spools of thread, buttons and some of her sewing tools.

Much to my regret, except for a few of the basic sewing and embroidery stitches which she did teach me, my mother did not feel it necessary for me to learn her craft. Because the apple does not fall far from the tree, I, nonetheless, inherited some of her talent and proclivity for working with my hands

I can thank my early exposure to my mother's avocation (and her genes), my deep admiration for her talent and my current passion for antique dolls and their authentic clothing for conspiring to guide me toward my own self-taught avocation of dressing antique dolls. In the beginning, when I first began collecting antique dolls, the struggle to properly dress them was great and the results were disappointing. As my own skills increased with experience— after much trial and error—I realized that I had learned valuable lessons that I could share with other collectors of antique dolls who know the basics of sewing and enjoy using these skills—even limited ones. I realized, too, that in many respects I could spare them the struggle and that I could even ensure them modest success. My many pattern portfolios and individual patterns for dressing antique dolls are the outgrowth of all this.

All the patterns included in this book have been designed to make sewing for antique dolls easy. Each garment has been researched for authenticity or based on original doll clothes of the period. All are constructed so that any amateur seamstress can create an attractive and suitable outfit for most kinds of antique dolls.

Each pattern set included is full size and ready to use. If you want to keep the patterns intact, simply copy them onto tracing paper. This type of paper is transparent and allows one to overlay the original pattern parts, trace them exactly and cut them apart. It is available at any art or drafting supply store. The use of a copy machine is not recommended because this kind of reproduction can shrink the image.

Inasmuch as old dolls were made in a profusion of sizes, it has been impossible to offer the patterns in sizes that would satisfy every collector's needs. To correct this deficiency, two versions of instructions for enlarging or decreasing pattern sizes are explained in detail and accompanied by diagrams that clarify the explanations. By following the set of instructions that work best for you, it is possible to duplicate any pattern part in the required size. In addition, easy to follow step-by-step sewing instructions, with all important details described, are presented in simple language.

Because synthetic fabrics were not used for doll clothing before World War I, do not use them when sewing for dolls made before that time. By the end of 1918, rayon was one of the early man-made textiles that achieved widespread popularity and it is certainly an appropriate choice for dolls made in the 1920s. Do not use any polyesters. If old fabrics are available, so much the better! It is crucial, however, to carefully examine these before using them to make certain that they have not been damaged. Otherwise, the hours of work may disintegrate before your eyes. When making a choice, relate the scale of the fabric's weight, texture and pattern to the size of the doll.

The use of old laces and trims do much to increase the illusion of authenticity. Although harsh colors may have been in vogue when the dolls were made, subtle, soft and restrained colors seem more appropriate for these fragile toys. The final ingredient required for success is your determination and willingness to invest your best effort in whatever endeavor you undertake. In return, the results will reward you.

Dolls of exactly the same height can and often do differ in their other body measurements. Therefore, it is wise to be aware of this possibility and to test the sizes of pattern parts before beginning work so that appropriate adjustments to them can be made. The more ambitious seamstress might even be willing to make a preliminary muslin of the garment so that it can be fit on the doll and necessary corrections made before cutting into a fabric that cannot be duplicated.

During the years that I have collected antique dolls, one of my fantasies has been to own a doll with her original trunk and wardrobe. As years passed and this dream remained unfulfilled, I began to think that it might be possible for me to create a wardrobe of my own making that would simulate in most respects an authentic one for a favorite doll. With the luxury of time to help me, I not only succeeded in fulfilling this goal, but I achieved it for more than one doll.

Among the many patterns included in this book are selections from three portfolios which focused on this endeavor, as well as additional patterns that incorporated results derived from this effort. It is my hope that other collectors with the same unrealized dreams can fulfill a similar ambition in a similar way.

The years of work that went into these projects have been greatly enhanced by my close association with two kind friends, Dorothy Dixon and Winnie Langley. Their generosity in sharing their collections, replete with original material, has been invaluable to me. Their friendship has enriched my life and, in some small measure, will do the same for others.

Evelyn Ackerman, 1993

HOW TO
ENLARGE OR DECREASE PATTERN SIZE

To Enlarge or Decrease Pattern Size — Method I

All patterns parts included in this book are full size. Although most of the patterns were made for specific dolls, many of which were small because of convenience factors, any of the patterns can be enlarged or even decreased in size so that the same garment can be created successfully for any doll of the same type.

You, the doll collector, may think this is too difficult to do. That, however, is not true. It does take a bit of time, but another hour or so is a small investment, especially when the effort results in an authentically styled garment for a cherished doll.

To change the pattern size, trace the individual pattern pieces onto paper. Around each pattern piece, draw an enclosing rectangle. Divide this into small equal squares, marking them in one direction numerically and in the other direction alphabetically to act as a kind of graph guide. Alongside this rectangle draw an identical rectangle (without squares). Extend the left hand vertical line to the height of the new pattern piece (measure the height for this pattern part on your doll). At the top of this line, draw a horizontal line to the point where it intersects the extension of the diagonal line (drawn from the bottom left corner to the top right corner). Then draw a line parallel to the left vertical to form the right vertical line. Join the bottom line to this. Divide this new rectangle into the same amount of squares as was done for the original pattern rectangle. Number and alphabetize to correspond. The pattern is then copied on the larger rectangle to fit the squares in an identical manner. Reverse the process to decrease the pattern size.

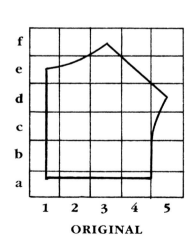

ORIGINAL

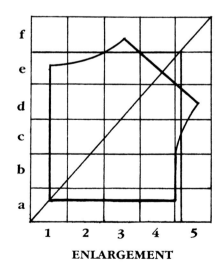

ENLARGEMENT

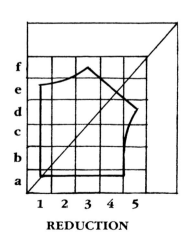

REDUCTION

To Enlarge or Decrease Pattern Size — Method II

The simplest method of enlarging or decreasing a pattern part is the one based on percentages. For example, if the pattern available is for an 8" doll, but the one to be dressed is 16", the enlargement is double or 100%. Enlarge each pattern part by first drawing a grid system on tracing paper (available at art supply stores) of equal squares that are, perhaps, 1/4" each (see ORIGINAL below). Place this over your original pattern part and trace it on the grid system. Then draw another grid system of equal squares that are 1/2" each (see ENLARGEMENT below). Using the ORIGINAL as a guide, draw the exact same pattern part on the 1/2" square grids by using the same points of contact and number of squares as points of reference to duplicate the pattern part on the larger grid system. It will automatically double its original size. When enlarging pattern parts for an 8" doll to ones for a 12" doll, the original pattern parts for the 8" doll could use 1/4" grids, but the squares for the enlargement would be 3/8" because the doll is only 50% larger. To decrease the size of a pattern part, the reverse should be done.

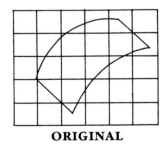

ORIGINAL

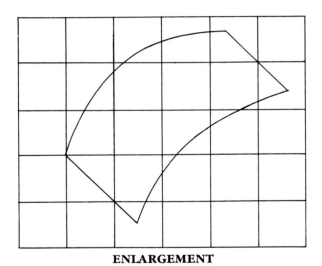

ENLARGEMENT

PATTERN NO. G-2
FOR A 14 INCH GIRL DOLL'S DRESS

General Instructions

• All pattern parts include 3/16" seams and hems, unless otherwise noted.

• Press all seams and hems as work proceeds.

• White cotton piqué or poplin best emulate the original doll dress, but other fabrics made from natural fibers, such as silk, taffeta, linen or light-weight wool, are suitable.

• If white cotton is used, trim with white cotton eyelet, no more than 1/2" wide. If other fabric is used, trim with either embroidered edging in related color or beige lace.

Bodice

1. Form two tuck pleats on fronts, with stitching toward front and fold toward side.

2. Optional: to insert narrow open-work tape (same as used on collar) alongside tuck pleats, cut left bodice front at short dotted line, folding each side of bodice front under so fold equals a half of width of open-work tape insert. Press folds. Connect each part of left front by sewing open-work tape in place. Repeat for right front.

3. With right sides together, sew center back of backs.

4. With right sides together, easing in fullness, sew side backs to backs.

5. With right sides together, sew side backs to fronts.

6. With right sides together, sew shoulder seams.

7. Turn under front facings of fronts and sew in place. Press. Overlap right side of front on top of left side of front, fitting to doll and allowing for buttons and buttonholes. Tack in place at bottom only.

8. Turn under top raw hem of half cuff and sew in place. Sew eyelet trim to top. Place half cuff over upper sleeve bottom, right sides up, and baste in place.

9. With right sides together, sew upper sleeve to under sleeve along one seam and then the other seam. Turn under bottom hem and sew in place.

10. With wrong side of bodice facing you and sleeve turned to right side, matching center of sleeve cap to shoulder seam, pin sleeve into armhole, easing in fullness for smooth fit. Sew in place. Repeat steps 8, 9 and 10 for other sleeve.

Skirt

1. Cut rectangle of dress fabric 4" wide x 31" long. Turn under one long raw edge, forming bottom hem. Sew in place. Press.

2. Form twelve box pleats, approximately 3/4" wide (finished size). Place on top of bodice at bottom, with skirt slightly longer in back than in front. Adjust as necessary. Then, with right sides together, sew center-back seam of skirt. Overlap skirt on top of bodice, matching center backs, and sew skirt to bodice with top edge remaining raw.

Sash, Center Back Panel, Collar

1. For waistline sash: cut rectangle of dress fabric 2" wide x 11" long. Turn under hems on all four sides and sew in place. Sew eyelet trim to sides and bottom of sash, pleating eyelet at corners.

2. Cut another rectangle of dress fabric 3" wide x 3" long. Turn under top and bottom hems and sew in place. Form two horizontal pleats, folding so pleats are facing up and finished size (height) is same as long waistline sash (not including eyelet trim). Baste pleats in place. Trim bottom with eyelet. Place this at center front of dress, top edge about 1/8"

Detail of back.

above waistline stitching. Tack in place at top edge. Overlap one side of long waistline sash on top of raw side of pleated center section, matching untrimmed hemmed top edges and pinning in place. Pin long waistline sash around back of bodice/skirt long center back panel rectangle and sew in place. Turn under short edges, pleating at center back at top of sash (thus, allowing sash to fit smoothly over pleated skirt). Overlap on other raw side of center front part of sash, with untrimmed hemmed tops matching. Adjust; then tack in place along untrimmed hemmed top edge of waistline sash.

3. For center back panel: cut rectangle of dress fabric 1-1/4" wide by 6-3/4" long. Cut another one 2" high x 3"

wide. Turn under long edges of long center back panel rectangle and sew in place. Turn under short edges of shorter rectangle and 3/4"-deep bottom hem and sew in place. Pleat this to fit bottom of long rectangle, with center having one vertical box pleat and a pleat on each side facing box pleat. Press and baste pleats in place. With right sides together, matching raw edges, sew short pleated center back panel to long center back panel. Press up and topstitch near seam. Beginning at top of one long side, sew eyelet trim to edge, continuing down side to bottom, across bottom (with eyelet pleated at corners), then up other side (not including neckline). Baste center back panel to dress at neckline, matching center of dress back to center of long center back panel. Tack center back panel in place on top of dress at center-back top of sash with two spaced-apart buttons. Also tack in place lower down.

4. Collar: turn under all edges, except neckline, to form hems. Sew in place. Sew narrow open trim (one that relates to eyelet trim—see front inserts) to hemmed edges. With right sides up, place collar against bodice, matching raw neckline edges and center backs. Baste in place. Cut bias strip 1/2" wide and 1/2" longer than neckline. With right sides together, place bias strip at neckline, matching raw neckline edges and allowing for side hems of bias strip. Sew in place (all parts as one). Press. Turn bias strip to wrong side; turn under hems and sew in place.

5. Sew four buttons and buttonholes at center-front opening, spacing about 1-1/6" apart.

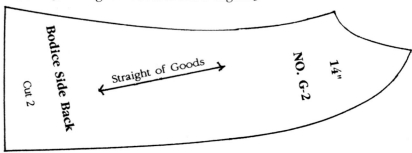

Bodice Side Back

Cut 2

Straight of Goods

14"

NO. G-2

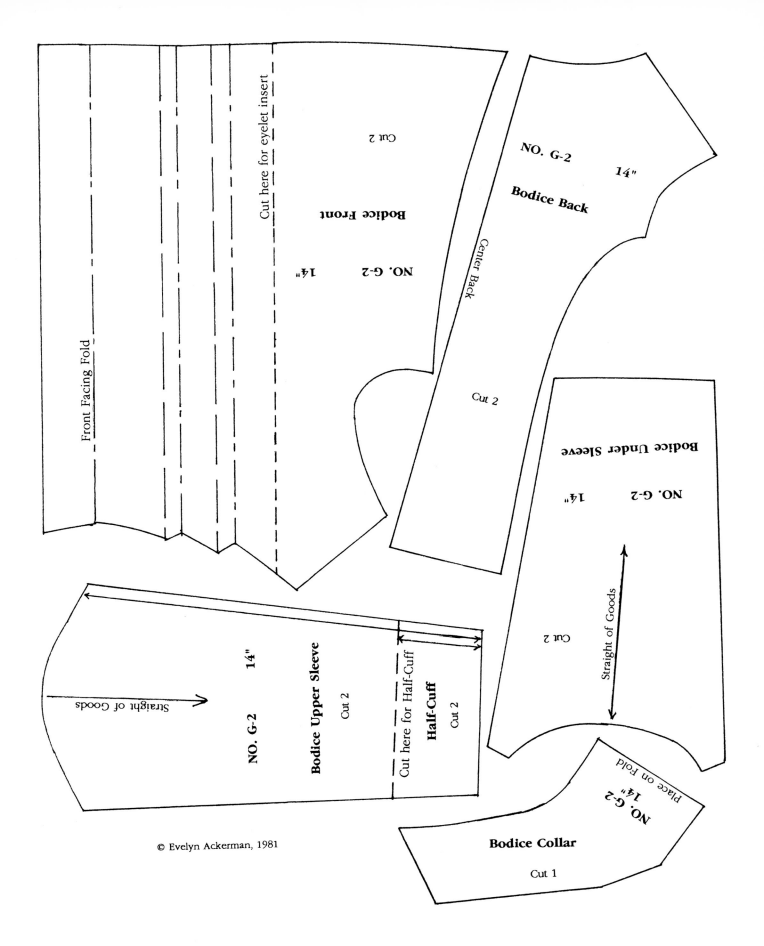

Cut 2

Bodice Front

Cut here for eyelet insert

NO. G-2   14"

Front Facing Fold

NO. G-2

Bodice Back

14"

Center Back

Cut 2

Bodice Under Sleeve

NO. G-2   14"

Cut 2

Straight of Goods

NO. G-2   14"

Bodice Upper Sleeve

Cut 2

Straight of Goods

Cut here for Half-Cuff

Half-Cuff

Cut 2

© Evelyn Ackerman, 1981

Place on Fold

NO. G-2   14"

Bodice Collar

Cut 1

PATTERN NO. G-3
FOR A 14 INCH GIRL DOLL'S DRESS

General Instructions

- All pattern parts include 1/4" seams and hems, unless otherwise noted.
- Press all seams and hems as work proceeds.
- Note that the lining is sewn separately from the dress fabric.
- All seams are piped, except for front edges, bottom hem and sleeve hem. The piping is made in the same way for all seams and should contrast with the color of the dress.
- This dress can be made from any fabric compatible with doll clothing of the late 19th century. The dress shown here was made from a wool challis that has an ecru background and a pale, scattered floral print. The piping is made from a maroon china silk. Trims include 1/4" wide maroon silk ribbon, card disk buttons covered with maroon silk thread and narrow lace. All elements, except the silk ribbon and cotton sewing thread, are old and suitable for the period.
- Other fabrics may be used, such as silk (especially a silk taffeta), lightweight wool, linen and cotton. Avoid any kind of synthetic fabric or trim.

Making and Using Piping

1. Measure the seams that need piping. Then cut a series of 3/8" wide bias strips, each 1/2" longer than the seam on which they will be used.

2. Since the finished piping is very narrow, use a heavy string to act as the cord. Place it in the center of the wrong side of each bias strip, then fold the strip in half (right side of fabric out); using a tiny running stitch, hand-stitch the length of the bias strip as close to the string-cord as possible.

3. The piping is placed against the right side of one side of each seam, matching raw edges. Then handstitch in place over the stitching next to the cord.

Lining

1. Cut out the lining pieces.

2. With right sides together, sew the center-back seam.

3. With right sides together, pin side to front, easing in fullness. Sew in place.

4. With right sides together, pin side to back, easing in fullness. Sew in place.

5. With right sides together, sew the shoulder seams. Set the lining aside temporarily.

Dress

1. Cut out the dress pieces. Note that the back pattern parts for the dress are cut to the pattern's dotted line, whereas the linings for these parts are cut the full length.

2. With right sides together, pin front to side (after piping is in place), easing in fullness. Sew in place. Measuring 3/4" from the front raw edge and 1" from the bottom raw edge, handstitch ribbon from raw neckline, down front, across bottom to back raw edge of side; miter corner of ribbon where the front edge turns to the side. Add a second row of ribbon in the same manner, leaving a 1/4" space between the two rows. Repeat for the other front and side pieces.

3. With rights sides together, sew center-back seam (after piping is in place). Matching raw seam edges, with right sides together, sew the top edge of the bottom back to the bottom edge of the back (no piping is inserted here).

4. To make the ruffles that go on the back of the dress, cut two 2" wide x 9" long rectangular pieces from the dress fabric. Hem one long side of each piece; to do so, turn under 1/8" of fabric, press it in place, then turn under 3/8" of fabric and baste hem. On the right side of each strip, place ribbon so it overlaps the top of the turned-under hem along its entire length; handstitch ribbon in place along long edges of both ruffle rectangles. Turn under the top raw edge of each strip and baste in place. Close to the

Side view, full figure.

top edge run gathering stitches. The top of one ruffle overlaps the seam connecting the dress's back and bottom back pieces; the other is placed so that its top edge is hidden by the upper ruffle and its bottom is just barely above the dress's finished hemline (allow 1/2" of fabric for bottom hem). Gather the two strips to fit across these locations and sew in place.

5. With right sides together, pin side to back, easing in fullness and catching in the raw seam edges of the gathered strips. Sew seams (after piping is in place).

6. With right sides together, sew shoulder seams (after piping is in place).

7. Using a small running stitch, sew piping to dress opening for sleeve; repeat at dress neckline.

8. With right sides together, matching front raw edges and seams, baste lining to dress, starting at the bottom-left front edge, up to the neckline, around the neckline, and down the right front edge to the bottom, leaving hemline raw. Sew; turn right side out.

9. Turn under bottom hem and turn in front edges of hem. Sew in place to lining only.

10. Sew piping to sleeve cuff, along top edge. Turn under narrow bottom hem and sew in place. Place ribbon so it overlaps the hem's stitching: sew it in place along both long edges. Gather the straight edge of the narrow lace and attach it to the bottom of the sleeve cuff, about 1/8" from the bottom edge on the underside. Repeat for other sleeve.

11. With right sides together, sew top of sleeve cuff to sleeve bottom, matching the raw edges of the sleeve and cuff seams. Repeat for other sleeve.

12. With right sides together, sew sleeve seam (after piping is in place). Repeat for other sleeve.

13. With the wrong side of the dress facing you and the sleeve turned to the right side, pin sleeve into armhole, matching sleeve seam piping to shoulder seam piping; ease in fullness. Handstitch in place. Repeat for other sleeve.

14. Forming ribbon in a "V," mitering bottom of "V," allowing for seams, place ribbon from raw top edges of the pocket to 1-1/2" from bottom of pocket's center. Handstitch in place along both edges of the ribbon. Sew a button to the ribbon at the bottom of the "V." Sew a ribbon bow just below the button. Repeat on other pocket.

15. Pipe all pocket edges. Gather the straight edge of lace and attach it to the underside of each pocket top, turning in raw ends.

16. Turn under all raw edges of each pocket and pin each pocket point to each of the dress's front/side seams, with the bottom of each pocket 1-3/4" above the edge of the finished dress hemline. Sew each pocket in place.

17. Sew seven evenly spaced buttons to right side of the dress front, 1/8" from the neckline and 3/16" from the front edge.

18. On the lining side of the right dress front, sew six evenly spaced hooks (attach to lining only). On the left dress front, sew corresponding eyes.

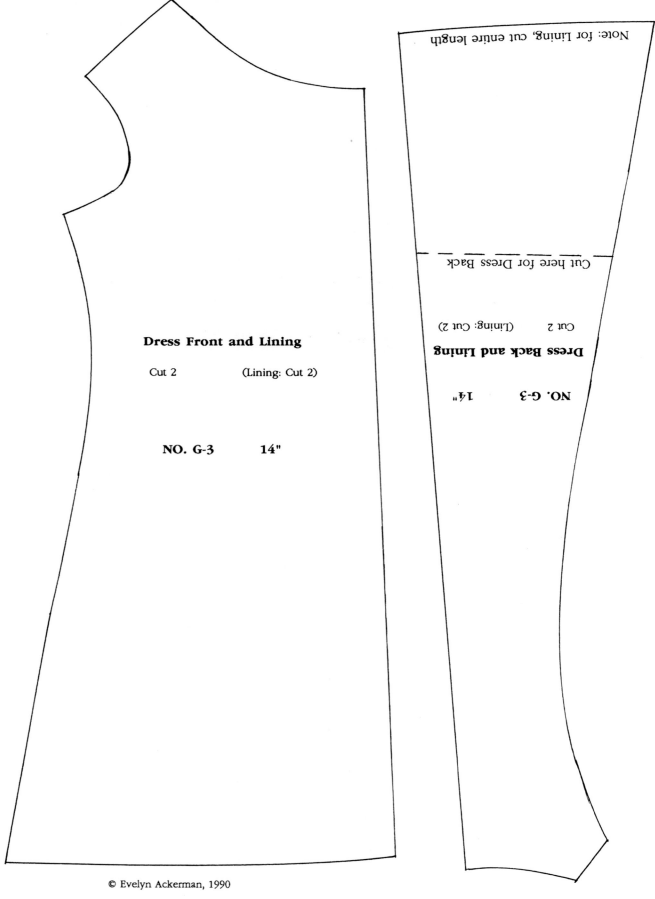

Dress Front and Lining

Cut 2   (Lining: Cut 2)

NO. G-3   14"

Note: for Lining, cut entire length

Cut here for Dress Back

Cut 2   (Lining: Cut 2)

Dress Back and Lining

NO. G-3   14"

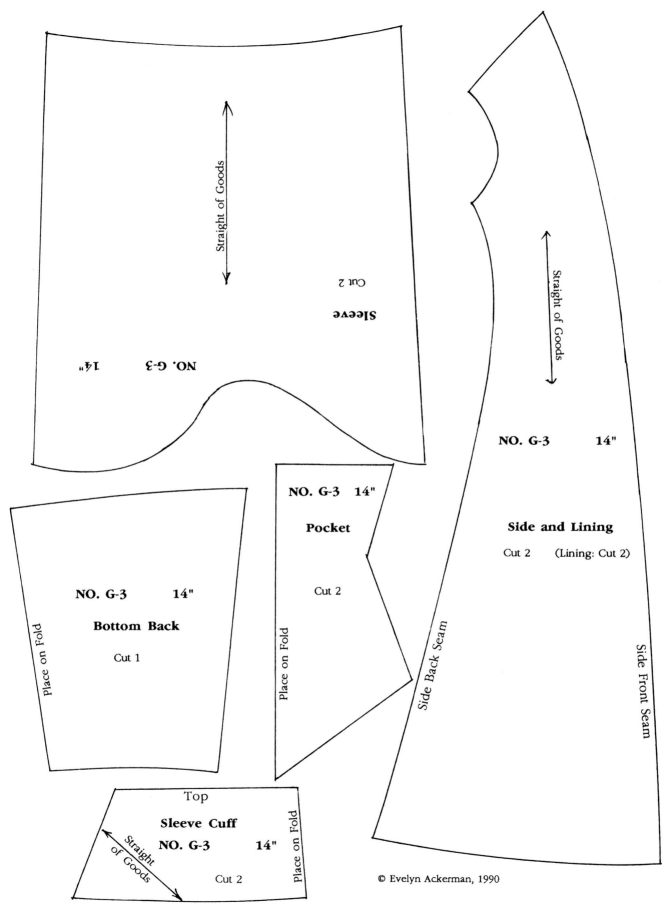

Straight of Goods

Sleeve
Cut 2

NO. G-3   14"

NO. G-3   14"

Straight of Goods

NO. G-3   14"

Side and Lining

Cut 2   (Lining: Cut 2)

NO. G-3   14"

Pocket

Cut 2

NO. G-3   14"

Bottom Back

Cut 1

Place on Fold

Place on Fold

Side Back Seam

Side Front Seam

Top

Sleeve Cuff

NO. G-3   14"

Cut 2

Place on Fold

Straight of Goods

© Evelyn Ackerman, 1990

17

Photograph: Bob Lopez

18

PATTERN NO. G-4
FOR A 14 INCH GIRL DOLL'S DRESS

General Instructions

• All pattern parts include 1/4" seams and hems, unless otherwise noted.

• Press all seams and hems as work proceeds.

• Dress bodice fabric can contrast in color with that of jacket, as well as be lightweight. Suitable fabrics for jacket and skirt are velvet, satin, taffetas, wool and silk. Lace, ribbon and braid trims are used. For illustrated garment, the bodice is made from ecru silk, the jacket/skirt from brown velvet and the sash from tan silk.

• Jacket cuffs, collar and lapels are lined.

Bodice

1. Baste and press front pleats in place. Secure across top and bottom.
2. With right sides together, sew center-back seam from bottom to notch. Press open and continue to press each side of 1/4" seam allowance. Handstitch opening in place.
3. With right sides together, sew sides to backs, easing in fullness.
4. With right sides together, sew sides to fronts.
5. With right sides together, sew shoulder seams.
6. From bodice fabric, cut bias strip 3/4" wide x 5-1/2" long. With right sides together, place bias strip at neckline; sew in place. Trim; clip curves; turn. Handstitch hem on wrong side.
7. Cut two bias strips 3/4" wide x 4-1/4" long. Repeat step 6 for armholes.
8. Tack large bow to center of bodice front at neckline.
9. At center-back opening, sew loops and buttons.

Skirt

1. Using same fabric as for jacket, cut rectangle 2" wide and 40" long. Turn under bottom hem and handstitch in place.

2. Form narrow knife pleats. Baste in place.
3. With right sides together, pin pleated skirt to bodice. Baste, then sew center-back seam of skirt. Sew skirt to bodice. Trim seam.

Jacket

1. Repeat steps 3, 4 and 5 of bodice for jacket.
2. Along shaped side of lapel, with right sides together, pleat and pin lace in place against lapel. Baste. With right side of lining facing down on lace and right side of lapel, sew lining in place (leave straight side open). Trim seam and turn lapel to right side. Repeat for other lapel.
3. At edge of lapel (near lace), on right side, sew braid trim in place.
4. Repeat jacket steps 2 and 3 for attaching lace, lining and braid to collar (with neckline left open so collar can be turned) and cuffs (with sides left open so cuffs can be turned).
5. At neckline, matching center backs, place collar (with right side up atop right side of garment). Baste. Repeat for each lapel, overlapping on each side of collar and matching bottom of each lapel to end of each diagonal cut of fronts.
6. Cut bias strip 3/4" wide and long enough to cover lapels and collar (to act as a front facing). With right sides together, place bias strip on top of lapels and collar. Sew in place. Trim; clip curves; turn; press. Handstitch bias facing in place on wrong side.
7. Along lower center-front edges and across bottom, turn under and handstitch hem in place.
8. Sew sleeve underarm seam. Sew side seam of laced and trimmed cuff. With right side of cuff against wrong side of sleeve, matching seams, sew bottom seam in place. Turn cuff away from sleeve; then turn sleeve to right

side. Turn cuff up and press. Repeat for other sleeve and cuff.
9. With wrong side of jacket facing you and the sleeve turned to the right side, put sleeve into armhole, matching underarm notch to underarm seam and top-center notch to shoulder seam. Pin in place, easing in fullness of the cap so fit is smooth. Sew in place. Trim seam. Repeat for other sleeve.
10. For sash, cut rectangle 4" wide x 14-3/4" long. Press under hem along both long edges. Fold rectangle in half (wrong sides together). Place pleated lace between the long open edges, allowing for 1/4" side seams to be closed at this time, and also slipstitching long open edges closed. Place braid (in same way as for lapels, collar and cuffs) above lace and sew in place. About 1/2" from top length of sash, form horizontal pleated fold. Tack in place. Pin sash to jacket, matching bottom edges, but tucking at front to fit center opening below lapels. Tack sash in place at several strategic points.
11. Sew hooks and eyes at center-front bottom opening. To one side of this, tack a large bow so it is centered when jacket is closed, but free of opening.

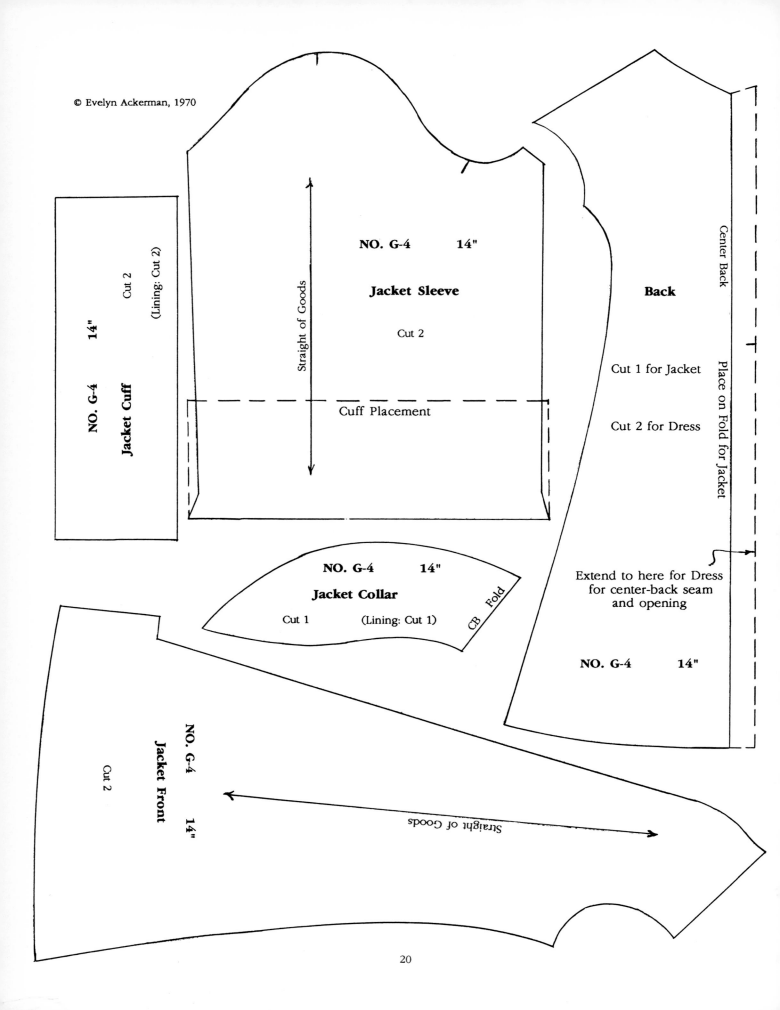

© Evelyn Ackerman, 1970

NO. G-4   14"

Jacket Sleeve

Cut 2

Straight of Goods

Cuff Placement

(Lining: Cut 2)

Cut 2

14"

NO. G-4

Jacket Cuff

NO. G-4   14"

Jacket Collar

Cut 1   (Lining: Cut 1)

CB Fold

Back

Cut 1 for Jacket

Cut 2 for Dress

Center Back

Place on Fold for Jacket

Extend to here for Dress
for center-back seam
and opening

NO. G-4   14"

NO. G-4

Jacket Front

14"

Cut 2

Straight of Goods

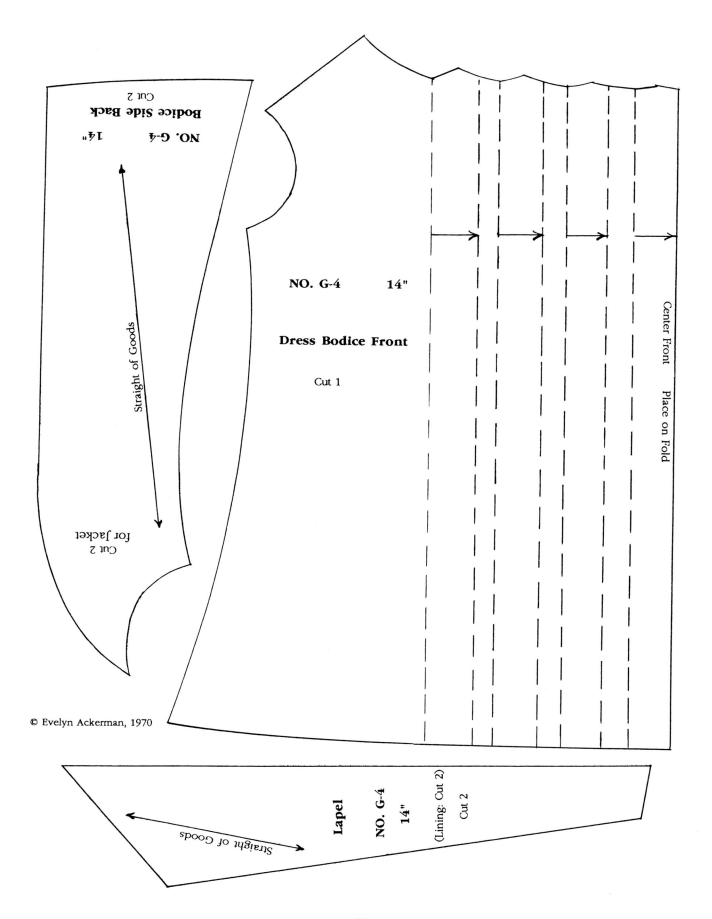

Bodice Side Back
Cut 2

NO. G-4   14"

Straight of Goods

Cut 2
for Jacket

NO. G-4   14"

Dress Bodice Front

Cut 1

Center Front   Place on Fold

© Evelyn Ackerman, 1970

Lapel

NO. G-4
14"

(Lining: Cut 2)

Cut 2

Straight of Goods

PATTERN NO. G-5
FOR A 12 INCH GIRL DOLL'S DRESS

General Instructions
• All pattern parts include 1/4" seams and hems, unless otherwise noted.
• Press all seams and hems as work proceeds.
• Suitable fabrics, either in solid colors or patterns, are lightweight wool, taffeta, silk, satin and velvet. Piping can be made from either contrasting colors or matching colors. As illustrated, the garment is made from a lightweight navy blue wool. The ecru lace trim has one scalloped edge and one straight edge. Ecru silk is used for the piping and wide ecru embroidered edging is used for the cuffs.

Dress
1. With right sides together, sew center back bottom to side back bottoms.
2. With right sides together, sew side back bottoms to front bottoms.
3. With right sides together, sew side backs to back, easing in fullness.
4. With right sides together, sew side backs to fronts.
5. With right sides together, sew shoulder seams.
6. To form piping, cut bias strip 5/8" wide x 26" long. Insert narrow cord (or string) at center of wrong side of bias strip, fold fabric in half (right sides out), and, using tiny running stitches, handstitch (or use machine zipper foot) as close to cord as possible.
7. Place raw edges of piping on top of all edges of bottom section, overlapping ends at an angle (to be hidden). Baste in place. Using machine zipper foot, as close to piping cord as possible, sew piping in place.
8. To make piping for front edges, cut two bias strips 5/8" wide and as long as front edges, following step 6. Place each piping strip on top of each front edge, matching raw edges. Using machine zipper foot, sew as close to piping cord as possible.

9. Cut six bias strips, 3/8" wide and as long as width of center-front insert (note this widens towards bottom). Fold in half, right side out. Topstitch straight edge of narrow lace over raw edge of folded bias strip. Place these in evenly spaced rows across center-front insert. Sew in place (over first topstitching).

10. With right sides together, using machine zipper foot, sew right front edge to center-front insert as close to piping cord as possible.

11. With right sides together, fit dress to doll and pin left front edge to center-front insert. Adjust for correct centering of center-front insert. Using machine zipper foot, sew from bottom up approximately 1/2" above piped bottom section. Remove pins.

12. For bottom pleating, cut dress fabric rectangle 1-1/4" wide x 42" long. Turn one long length under for hem and handstitch in place. Form knife pleats along entire length, allowing for center-back seam. Baste in place. Fit raw edge of pleats to lower edge of garment, adjusting size. With right sides together, sew center-back seam of pleated section. With right sides together, matching center backs, using machine zipper foot, sew pleats to dress as close to piping cord as possible.

13. With right sides together, sew collar lining to collar, leaving neckline edge open. Trim and clip seam. Turn and press. With both right sides facing up, matching center backs, baste collar to neckline. Cut bias strip 5/8" wide and slightly longer than entire neckline. With right sides together, matching raw edges and matching collar ends to tops of piped fronts, sew bias strip to entire neckline, leaving left front and center-front insert unattached. Trim seam and clip curves. Turn bias strip to wrong side and turn in raw ends. Handstitch bias strip hem in place. If desired, add bias strip/lace combination (as on center-front insert, step 9) near and around curved bottom edge of collar.

14. With right sides together, sew sleeve underarm seam. With right sides together, sew cuff seam (wide lace or embroidered edging can be used). With right side of cuff facing wrong side of sleeve, sew bottom edge. Trim, turn to outside and press. Repeat for other sleeve and cuff.

15. With wrong side of bodice facing you and the sleeve turned to the right side, put the sleeve into the armhole, matching underarm notch to underarm seam and top-center notch to shoulder seam. Pin in place, easing in cap fullness for smooth fit. Sew in place. Trim seam. Repeat for other sleeve.

16. Along inside edge of left front and center-front insert, sew hooks and eyes to fasten.

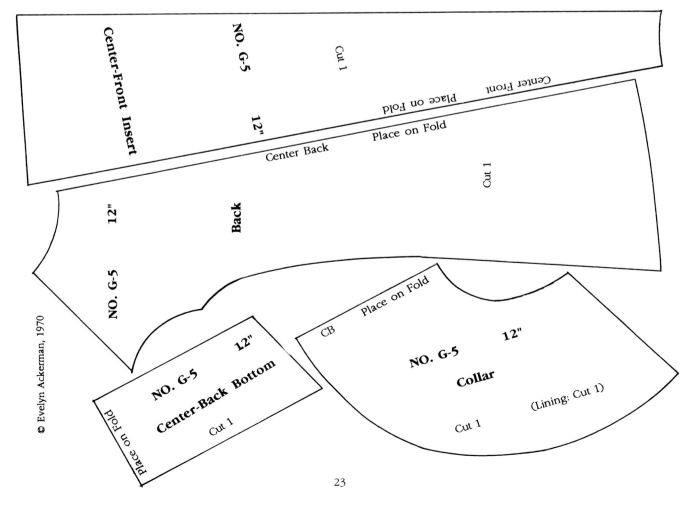

23

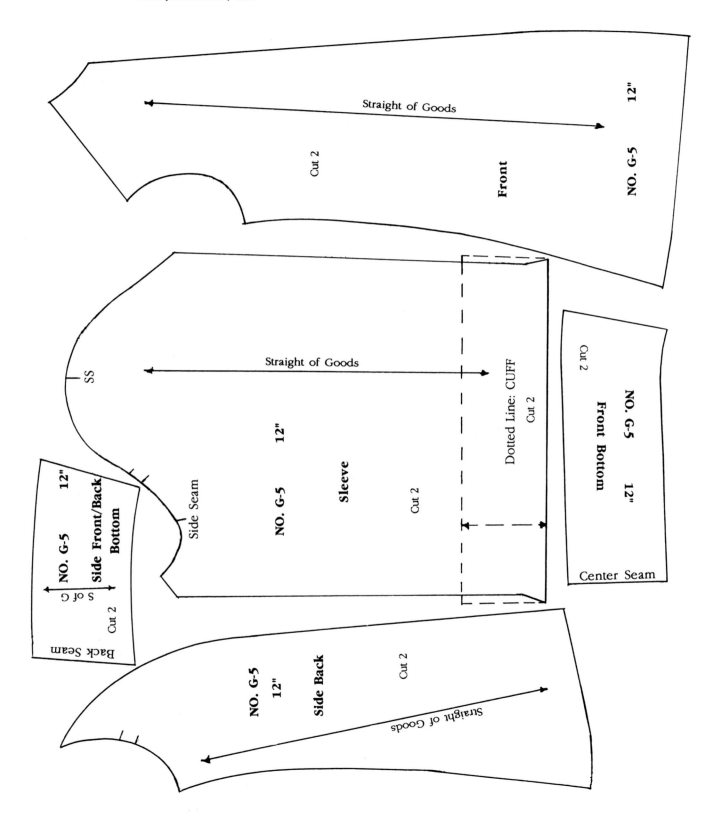

24

PATTERN NO. G-6
FOR A 12 INCH GIRL DOLL'S DRESS

General Instructions

- All pattern parts include 1/4" seams and hems, unless otherwise noted.
- Press all seams and hems as work proceeds.
- Many fabrics made from natural fibers are suitable for making this dress. Especially appropriate are silks and lightweight cottons, such as dotted swiss, voiles and cambric.

Bodice

1. For two belt sections, cut two pieces of dress fabric and two pieces of lining fabric, 2" wide x 14" long. For one belt, with right sides together, sew one end in point and both long edges of dress fabric to lining fabric, leaving other end open. Trim seam and corners; turn to right side and press. Repeat for other belt section.

2. Pin bodice front tucks into place. Sew (close to edge nearest front) by using tiny running stitches.

3. About 1/4" from open end of one belt section, run two or three parallel lines of tiny running stitches about 1/16" apart from top to bottom of width. Gather to shirr. At open end of belt, at center, tack a narrow, folded pleat into position. Repeat for other belt section.

4. At both side seams of bodice front, with right sides together, baste belt sections to front between notches, matching open ends of belt sections to raw side seams of front.

5. With right sides together, sew center-back seam from bottom to notch. Press open, including portion of center-back opening not sewn. Hand-stitch center-back hems in place.

6. With right sides together, sew bodice side backs to bodice back, easing in fullness.

7. For top back pleated section, cut one piece of dress fabric 2-1/4" wide x 17" long. Press under 1/4" hems top and bottom of top back rectangle. Handstitch bottom hem in place. Baste top hem. Form knife pleats along length of top back rectangle, allowing for 1/4" seams on each side. Press and baste in place. With right sides out, fit to back just beneath position of belt, matching raw seam edges. Sew in place by handstitching close to top edge.

8. With right sides together, avoiding catching in belt sections, sew bodice side backs to bodice front.

9. With right sides together, sew shoulder seams.

Skirt

1. For skirt, cut dress fabric rectangle 2-3/4" wide x 33-1/2" long. Press under 1/4" bottom hem of skirt rectangle. Handstitch bottom hem in place. Form knife pleats along entire length, allowing for center-back seam. Press and baste pleats firmly in place.

2. With right sides together, fit skirt pleat to bodice just beneath top back pleat, pinning at first to check size and make necessary adjustments. With right sides together, sew center-back seam of skirt pleats. With right sides together, matching center backs, sew skirt pleats to bodice bottom (topstitch raw seam edge as close to seam as possible).

Another view.   Photograph: Bob Lopez

Bodice

1. For front bodice trim, use either lace or lace and beading lace/ribbon combination. Starting below neckline, baste four evenly spaced rows of narrow, straight-edged lace between bodice front tucks (see pattern). Handstitch in place. Starting at raw neckline edge, sew lace parallel to right-hand tucks, covering raw edges of four rows of lace, continue attaching lace above skirt pleating, mitering both right and left lace corners, and up left-hand side parallel to tucks to raw neckline edge.

2. Cut bias strip 3/4" wide x 6" long, using dress fabric. With right sides together, sew to neckline. Trim and clip seam. Turn to wrong side, forming narrow neckband and allowing for hem on wrong side. Press. Handstitch bias hem on wrong side.

3. Sew buttonhole loops and buttons to center-back opening.

4. Turn under sleeve bottom hem. Sew lace trim to bottom of sleeve. With right sides together, sew sleeve's underarm seam. Repeat for other sleeve.

5. With wrong side of bodice facing you and the sleeve turned to the right side, put the sleeve into the armhole, matching center top to shoulder seam and underarm notch to side seam. Pin in place, easing in cap fullness for smooth fit. Sew sleeve in place. Trim seam. Repeat for other sleeve.

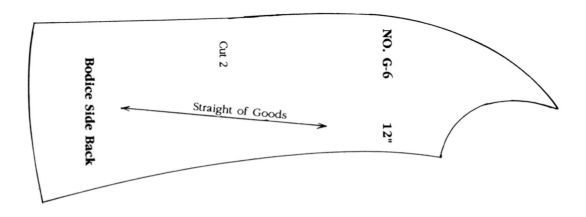

Bodice Side Back

Cut 2

Straight of Goods

NO. G-6

12"

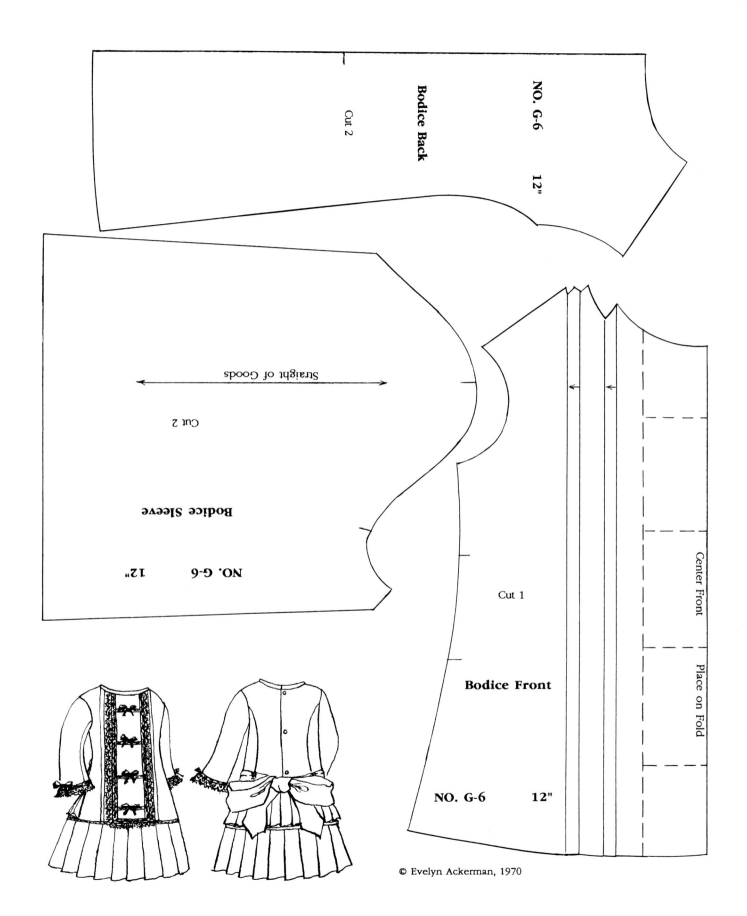

NO. G-6   12"

Bodice Back

Cut 2

Straight of Goods

Cut 2

Bodice Sleeve

NO. G-6   12"

Center Front

Place on Fold

Cut 1

Bodice Front

NO. G-6   12"

© Evelyn Ackerman, 1970

27

PATTERN NO. G-7
FOR A 9 INCH GIRL DOLL'S DRESS

General Instructions

• All pattern parts include 1/4" seams and hems, unless otherwise noted.

• Press all seams and hems as work proceeds.

• Any fabric made from a natural fiber that is soft and pliable, as well as lightweight, is suitable. Deep colors, such as maroon, with contrasting lace are most effective in combination with very narrow antique gold braid.

Dress

1. With right sides together, sew yoke back to yoke front at shoulders.

2. Gather top of skirt front. With right sides together, fit to yoke front. Sew in place.

3. Gather tops of skirt backs. With right sides together, fit to yoke backs. Sew in place.

4. With right sides together, sew center-back seam from bottom to notch. Press open, including center-back hems. Handstitch center-back hems in place.

5. With right sides together, sew side seams.

6. With right sides together, sew collar lining to collar, leaving neckline open. Trim seam; clip curves; turn to right side; press. Baste braid in place on collar, then handstitch.

7. With right sides up, baste collar at neckline, matching raw edges. Cut bias strip from dress fabric 5/8" wide x 5" long and place on top of collar at neckline, right sides together. Baste, then sew collar and bias strip (tucking in bias edges) to neckline. Trim seam; clip curves; press. Turn bias strip to wrong side and handstitch hem in place.

8. Attach lace wide enough to cover sleeve cap from collar edge, starting at bottom left back of collar and finishing at bottom right back. Pleat lace slightly

to give some fullness and allow for shaping to collar. Handstitch in place.

9. With right sides together, sew sleeve bottom to sleeve bottom lining along lower edges. Turn to right side; press. About 3/8" from bottom, handstitch braid in place. Repeat for other sleeve bottom.

10. Sew tiny running stitches along bottom edge of upper sleeve. With right sides together, matching raw edges, gather and adjust bottom edge of upper sleeve to fit top of sleeve bottom. Sew in place. Repeat for other sleeve.

11. Sew tiny running gathering stitches to sleeve cap. Sew sleeve underarm seam. Repeat for other sleeve.

12. With wrong side of bodice facing you and the sleeve turned to the right side, put the sleeve into the armhole, matching underarm sleeve seam with side seam and cap center to shoulder seams. Gather sleeve cap to fit armhole opening. Pin and adjust gathers. Sew in place. Trim seam. Repeat for other sleeve.

13. Fit dress to doll and turn under bottom hem to desired length. Pin and handstitch in place.

14. At center-back opening, sew buttonhole loops and buttons.

NO. G-7   9"

Skirt Front

Cut 1

Center Front   Place on Fold

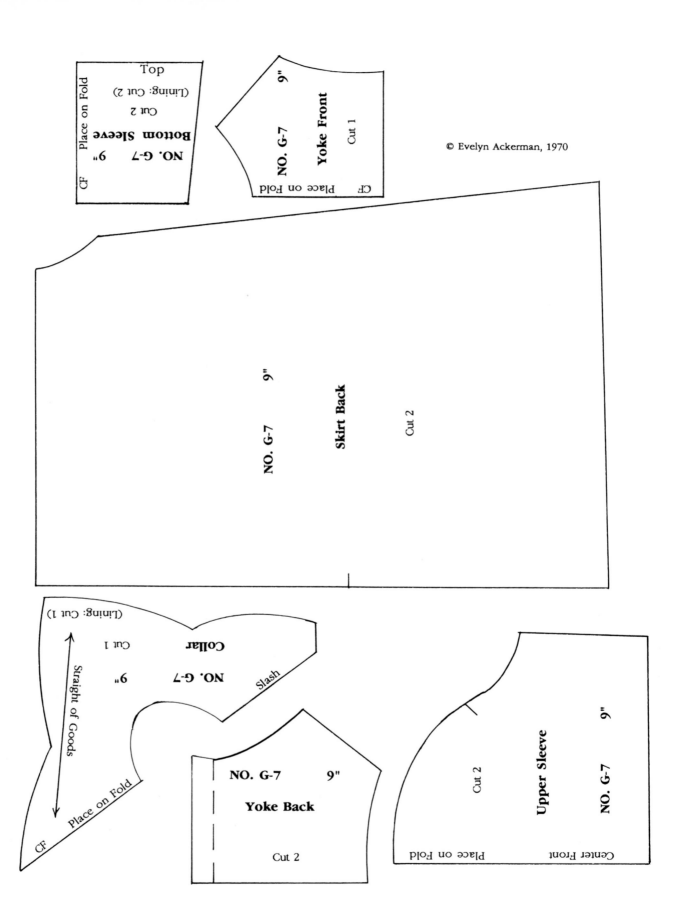

Top
Place on Fold
(Lining: Cut 2)
Cut 2
Bottom Sleeve
NO. G-7 9"
CF

9"
NO. G-7
Yoke Front
Cut 1
Place on Fold
CF

© Evelyn Ackerman, 1970

NO. G-7 9"

Skirt Back

Cut 2

(Lining: Cut 1)
Cut 1
Collar
NO. G-7 9"
Slash
Straight of Goods
Place on Fold
CF

NO. G-7 9"
Yoke Back
Cut 2

Upper Sleeve
NO. G-7 9"
Cut 2
Place on Fold
Center Front

PATTERN NO. G-10
FOR AN 11 INCH GIRL DOLL'S DRESS

General Instructions

• All pattern parts include 1/4" seams and hems, unless otherwise noted.

• Press all seams and hems as work proceeds.

• Use only a soft, limp fabric, such as washed muslin. Use only 1/8" wide ribbon that either matches the fabric or is closely related in color. Lace, too, is required. The best colors are white, ecru, pale pink or pale blue. The trims should be either white or ecru.

Yoke and Bodice

1. Baste five pieces of ribbon (start at center and work towards side seams) to front yoke (right side of ribbon facing up on right side of fabric). Ribbon is placed vertically from raw edge of neckline to bottom of yoke. Sew in place.

2. Repeat, attaching ribbon in same way to back yoke, with two pieces on each side.

3. With right sides together, sew shoulder seams.

4. Sew tiny running stitches to top of bodice front. Gather. Fit to front yoke. With right sides together, sew bodice front to front yoke. Topstitch seam as close to seam edge as possible.

5. Sew tiny running stitches to bottom of bodice front, but only as marked on pattern. Gather until bodice front assumes shape of straight-sided square. Secure gathers in place.

6. Repeat steps 4 and 5 for bodice back, gathering and attaching to back yoke in same way as for front parts.

7. Press under both sides of center-back opening hems and sew in place.

8. Bend under hem at neckline of yoke. Then press and baste in place. Topstitch ribbon to neckline, matching top edge of ribbon to top edge of neckline.

9. Turn under bottom hem of lower sleeve. After sewing as close to edge as possible, place ribbon along this bottom edge, with ribbon extending a touch below bottom hem. Baste and then sew in place

10. Turn under bottom hem of upper sleeve and sew as close to edge as possible. Place ribbon along this bottom edge, with ribbon extending a touch below bottom hem. Baste in place. Sew another row of ribbon, about 1/4" above this on upper sleeve.

11. Gather top edge of lower sleeve. Fit to upper sleeve and topstitch upper sleeve in place over lower sleeve (across basting thread of ribbon on bottom).

12. Add lace along lower edge of sleeve. Handstitch in place.

13. With right sides together, sew sleeve underarm seam. With wrong side of bodice facing you and sleeve turned to right side, put sleeve into armhole, matching underarm seam to side seam and center of sleeve top to shoulder seam. Ease into armhole for smooth fit, first pinning while adjusting, then sewing in place. Trim seam. Repeat steps 9-13 for other sleeve.

Skirt

1. On both lower bottom back (two pieces) and lower bottom front (one piece), turn under bottom hems. Press. Sew at bottom edge.

2. Starting at bottom edge, with ribbon extending a touch below bottom hem, baste ribbon in evenly spaced bands to lower bottom front, repeating for lower bottom backs. Sew in place only at upper edge of ribbon.

3. Turn under hems of upper bottom front and two pieces of upper bottom backs. Sew in place. Do not yet attach ribbon along this hemline edge. Instead, measure correct space for ribbon that bands above this. Baste ribbon in place and then sew only along upper edge of ribbon.

4. Sew tiny running stitches to top edge of lower bottom front, gather and fit under upper bottom front hem. Topstitch in place.

5. Sew tiny running stitches to top edge of upper bottom front, gather and fit to bodice front. With right sides together, sew upper bottom front to bodice front.

6. Sew center-back seam below back bodice and yoke opening. Press open.

7. Overlap left bodice back over right bodice back. Tack in place 1/8" above bottom edge.

8. Repeat steps 4 and 5 for lower bottom back, for upper bottom back, for bodice back.

9. With right sides together, sew side seams, matching bands of ribbons.

10. At seam line of upper bottom and lower bottom sections, topstitch a band of ribbon around garment, starting at left center back and ending at right center back, finishing by overlapping and tucking under 1/8" hem of ribbon. Tack in place.

11. Repeat step 10 at waistline seam.

12. Add lace (top edge of lace is under garment edge) to entire bottom hem and also at neckline, using very narrow lace at neckline. Handstitch in place.

Bodice Overlay

1. Turn under hem along all edges, clipping curves. Press. Sew close to edge.

2. Baste ribbon in place along entire bottom edge. Sew in place. Baste ribbon about 1/2" above this, but do not follow this row down the "tails." Instead, miter into square shape across center section. Sew in place.

3. Starting at underside edge of bottom of center back, add lace to entire bottom edge of bodice overlay. Handstitch in place.

4. Baste top edge of bodice overlay to yoke. Sew in place.

5. Starting at left center-back opening and ending at right center-back opening, place ribbon over top edge of bodice overlay. Topstitch in place.

6. At center back, sew three buttonholes and three buttons.

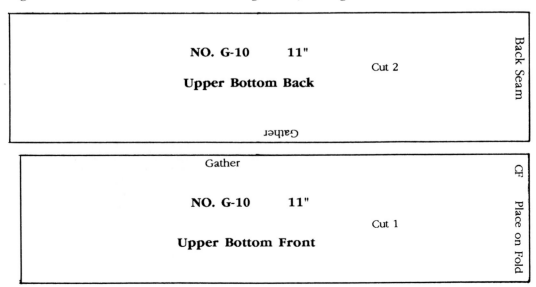

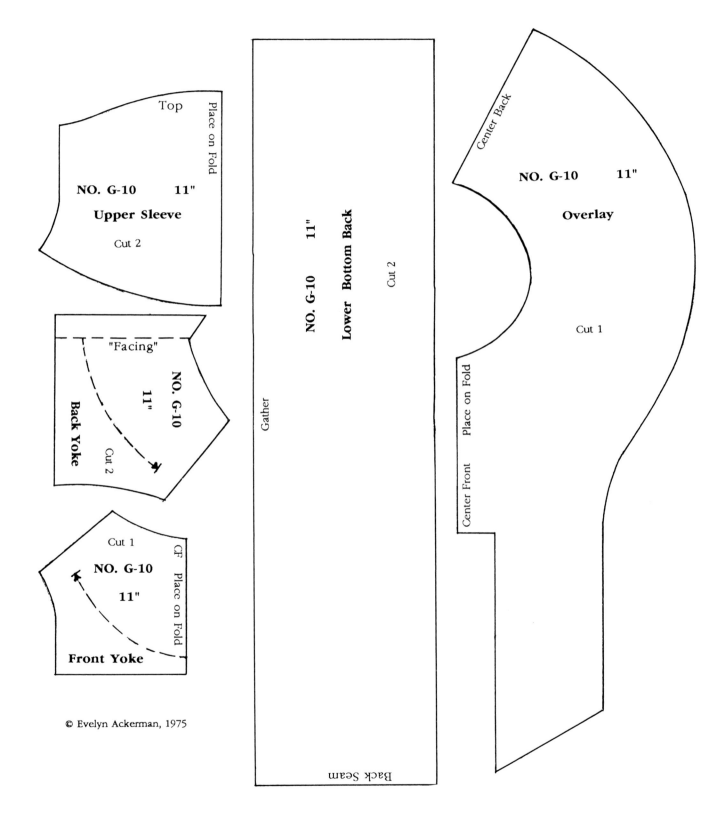

Top

Place on Fold

NO. G-10　　11"

Upper Sleeve

Cut 2

"Facing"

NO. G-10

11"

Back Yoke

Cut 2

Cut 1

NO. G-10

11"

CF　Place on Fold

Front Yoke

© Evelyn Ackerman, 1975

Gather

NO. G-10　　11"

Lower　Bottom　Back

Cut 2

Back Seam

Center Back

NO. G-10　　11"

Overlay

Cut 1

Center Front

Place on Fold

33

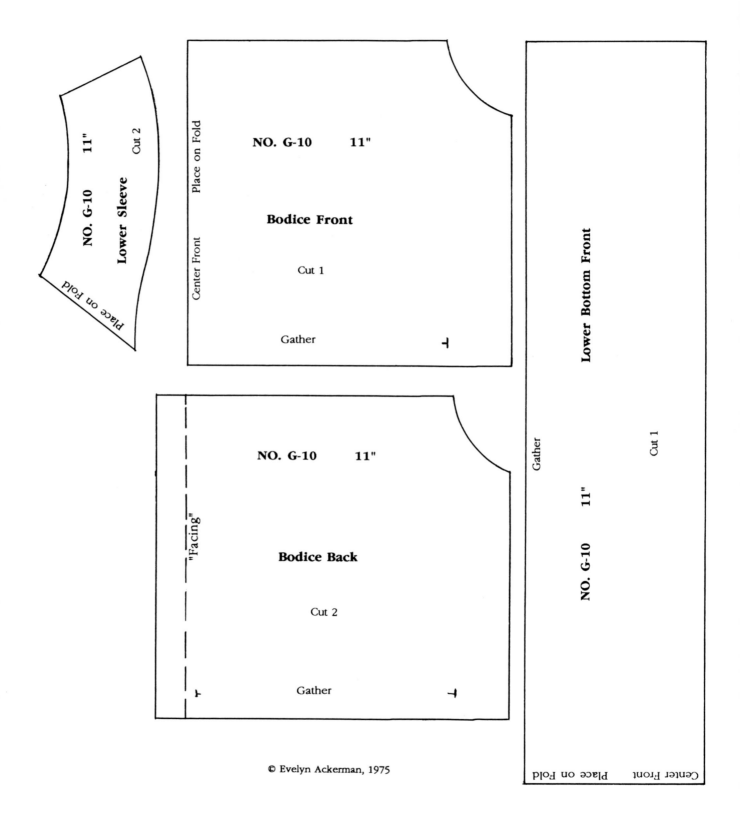

NO. G-10   11"

Lower Sleeve   Cut 2

Place on Fold

Place on Fold

Center Front

NO. G-10   11"

Bodice Front

Cut 1

Gather

"Facing"

NO. G-10   11"

Bodice Back

Cut 2

Gather

Gather

Lower Bottom Front

Cut 1

NO. G-10   11"

Center Front   Place on Fold

© Evelyn Ackerman, 1975

34

PATTERN NO. G-12
FOR A 20 INCH GIRL DOLL'S DRESS

General Instructions

• All pattern parts include 1/4" seams and hems, unless otherwise noted.

• Press all seams and hems as work proceeds.

• Finely woven, soft, pliable fabrics are most suitable, such as batiste, gauze, voile, dotted swiss. For most attractive results, colors selected should be white or pale pastels, with lace in colors that blend with fabric color. Ribbon must be narrow, less than 1/4" wide if possible.

Skirt

1. From dress fabric, cut two rectangles 9" wide x 9-1/2" long (skirt backs) and one rectangle 9" wide x 21" long (skirt front).

2. For both skirt front and skirt backs, form pleats that are about 3/8" wide, facing pleats toward center. Allow for side seams and center-back seams. Press at top. Baste in place. (Actual dimensions must be adjusted to fit individual doll's waist, allowing for thickness of undergarments.)

3. With right sides together, sew skirt front to skirt backs at side seams.

4. Optional: about one-third of the way up from the bottom, overlay skirt with lace and/or beading lace to match that of yoke. Place narrow ribbon along top and bottom edge of lace and topstitch in place (along both edges of ribbon). An additional length of ribbon can be placed about one-half inch above this and topstitched in place.

Yoke

1. Piece together lace and beading lace with ribbon inserts, both wide and long enough to fit pattern parts of yoke front and yoke backs. Overlay seams with ribbon, topstitching each ribbon edge. Cut to fit pattern parts.

2. To prevent stretching of neck opening, stitch along entire neck opening about 1/16" from edge.

3. With right sides together, sew shoulder seams.

Bodice

1. Cut remaining pattern parts from dress fabric. Handstitch tiny running stitches along both top and bottom edges of bodice front and bodice backs.

2. Gather top edge of bodice front to fit yoke front. With right sides together, matching centers, sew bodice front to yoke front. Press up. Topstitch on yoke at seam edge. Repeat for bodice backs and yoke backs.

3. With right sides together, sew side seams.

4. Gather bottom of bodice front to fit skirt front, matching sides and center fronts. With right sides together, sew in place. Press up. Topstitch on bodice at waist seam edge. Repeat for bodice backs and skirt backs.

5. With right sides together, sew front to backs at side seams.

6. Overlay waist seam with narrow ribbon and topstitch in place along both edges.

7. With right sides together, sew center-back seam from bottom up approximately 6". Press open, including center-back opening. Handstitch center-back opening hems in place.

8. Handstitch tiny running stitches along sleeve cap and sleeve bottom. With right sides together, sew underarm seam of sleeve. Repeat for other sleeve.

9. Gather sleeve cap. With wrong side of bodice facing you and sleeve turned to right side, matching sleeve top center to shoulder seam and sleeve underarm seam to bodice side seam, place sleeve in armhole. Adjust gathers to fit, pinning in place. Sew in place. Repeat for other sleeve.

10. With right sides together, sew side seam of each sleeve band.

11. Gather sleeve bottom to fit sleeve band. With right sides together, match-

ing seams and centers, sew sleeve to sleeve band. Bend sleeve band in half, allowing for underside hem. Handstitch hem in place. Repeat for other sleeve.

12. Topstitch ribbon, placed along sleeve band seam, along top edge only. Gather lace and baste in place on lower edge of sleeve band under ribbon. Handstitch lace side seam, matching it to sleeve side seam. Topstitch bottom edge of ribbon over lace. Repeat for other sleeve.

Bertha Collar and Neckband

1. Pattern is maximum size of bertha collar. This may be reduced by adjusting width of laces and fabrics if more of gathered bodice is to show. When miters are joined, lace, fabric, ribbon must match. The bertha collar is composed of the following parts: (a) strip of fabric (top), (b) lace and/or beading lace with ribbon insert, (c) strip of

fabric, (d) lace with scalloped edge (bottom). These parts are first joined together (machine or handstitch). Narrow ribbon is placed over the sewn edges and topstitched in place along both edges. Fit and cut to pattern.

2. With right sides together, sew bertha collar fronts to bertha collar centers (mitered joint). Press and trim seams. With right sides together, sew bertha collar backs to bertha collar centers. Press and trim seams.

3. Turn under top edge of bertha collar; press in place. Beginning at yoke front, center bottom, then continuing over shoulder, and finishing at yoke back center bottom, sew in place. Overlay top edge with narrow ribbon, topstitching in place along both edges.

4. Cut bias strip 3/4" wide x 8" long for narrow neckband. With right sides together, baste bias strip to neckline, allowing raw ends to be turned into

back hem. Sew in place. Press. Bend to wrong side, forming narrow neckband and allowing for hem. Handstitch hem on wrong side.

5. Optional: trim neckband with narrow ribbon and gathered lace.

6. Fit dress to doll and turn under bottom hem of skirt and handstitch in place.

7. Sew hooks and eyes to centerback opening.

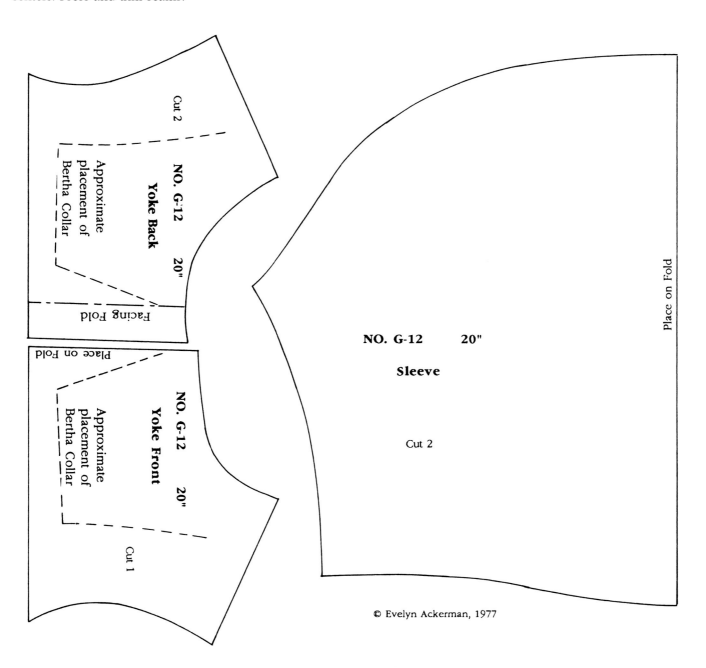

© Evelyn Ackerman, 1977

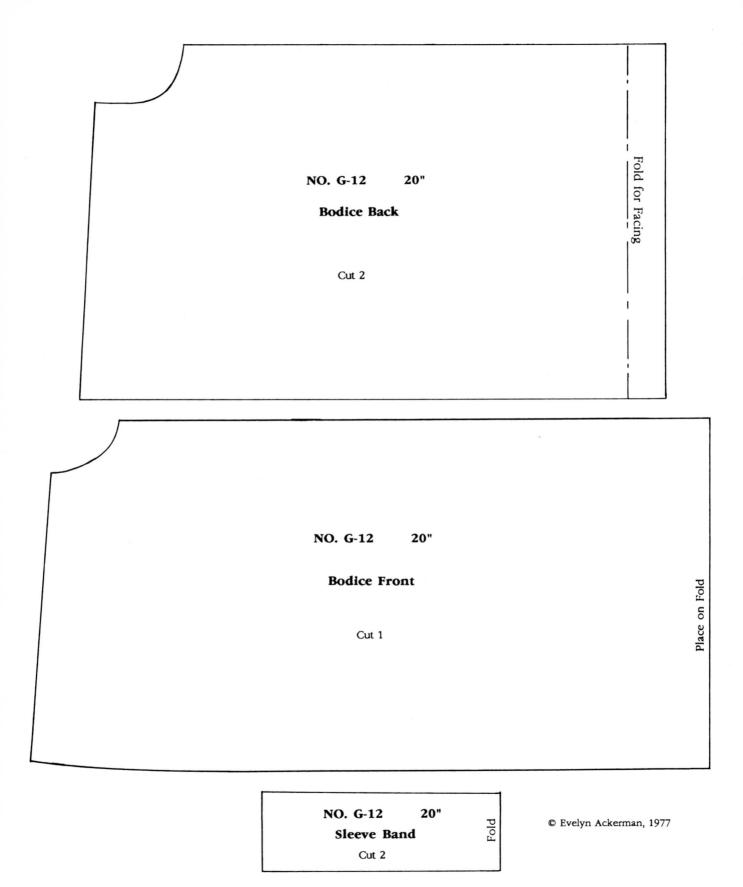

NO. G-12   20"

Bodice Back

Cut 2

Fold for Facing

NO. G-12   20"

Bodice Front

Cut 1

Place on Fold

NO. G-12   20"

Sleeve Band

Cut 2

Fold

© Evelyn Ackerman, 1977

38

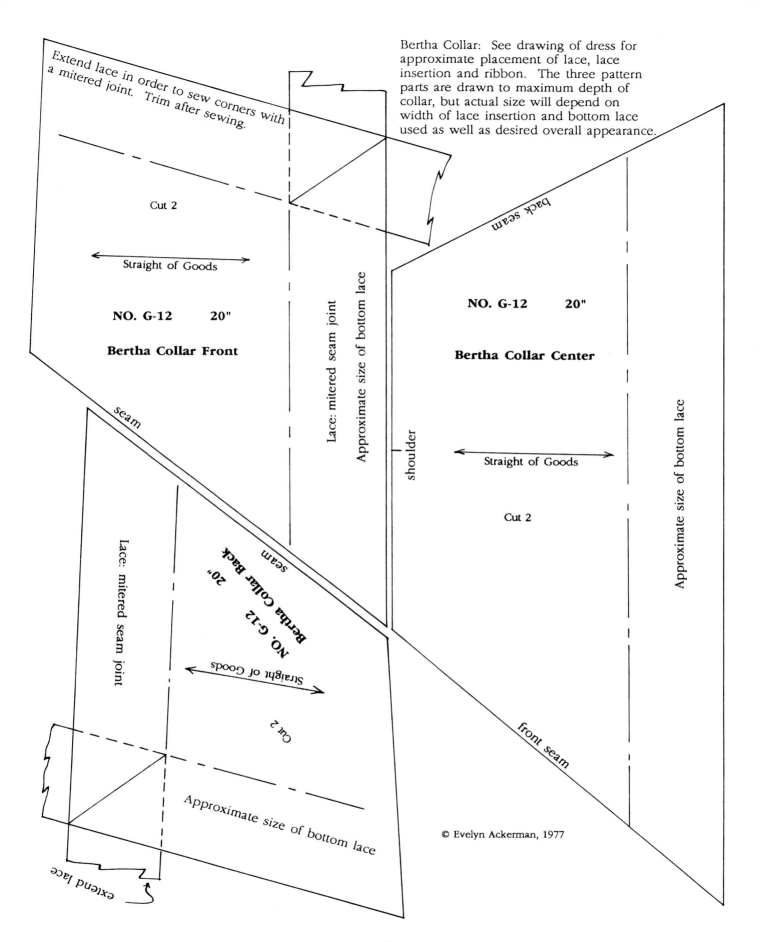

Extend lace in order to sew corners with a mitered joint. Trim after sewing.

Bertha Collar: See drawing of dress for approximate placement of lace, lace insertion and ribbon. The three pattern parts are drawn to maximum depth of collar, but actual size will depend on width of lace insertion and bottom lace used as well as desired overall appearance.

Cut 2

Straight of Goods

NO. G-12   20"

Bertha Collar Front

Lace: mitered seam joint

Approximate size of bottom lace

back seam

NO. G-12   20"

Bertha Collar Center

Straight of Goods

Cut 2

shoulder

Approximate size of bottom lace

seam

Lace: mitered seam joint

seam

NO. G-12   20"

Bertha Collar Back

Straight of Goods

Cut 2

Approximate size of bottom lace

front seam

extend lace

© Evelyn Ackerman, 1977

PATTERN NO. G-14
FOR AN 8-1/2 INCH GIRL DOLL'S DRESS

General Instructions
- All pattern parts include 1/8" seams and hems, unless otherwise noted.
- Press all seams and hems as work proceeds.
- Finely woven, lightweight fabrics (for example, cambric and other cottons, silk taffeta, cotton-backed satin, satin, linen) are suitable. Fabrics with solid colors or small patterns can be used. Narrow lace with one scalloped edge is required.

Dress
1. With right sides together, sew side backs to back.

2. Cut rectangle of dress fabric 2-1/4" wide x 13-1/2" long. Form eight box pleats, approximately 1/2"-5/8" wide. Press and baste in place along top edge. With right sides together, sew pleated section to lower edge of back section.

3. With right sides together, sew fronts to side fronts.

4. With right sides together, sew fronts to back at side seams.

5. Fit dress to doll and turn under bottom hem. Handstitch in place. Then, repress bottom back box pleats.

6. Cut duplicate parts of side fronts (bottom at dotted line) and side back. With right sides together, sew side seams.

7. For piping, cut long bias strip from dress fabric (or contrasting color), 1/4" wide and slightly longer than edge of sewn-together side fronts and side backs from neckline to neckline. Place heavy string on wrong side at center. Bend bias strip in half, right sides out. Handstitch tiny running stitch as close to cord as possible, enclosing cord. Repeat for length of top edge of side pockets, cuffs, and collar outside edge.

8. Pipe top edge of side pocket by placing right sides of piping and side pocket together, matching raw edge of piping and top of side pocket. Hand-

stitch in place as close to cord as possible. Turn raw top edge under and press. Add lace, handstitching to underside of piping at top of side pocket. Repeat for other side pocket.

9. Pin side pocket in place at bottom of side front/side back overlay, matching raw edges. With long piping, pipe entire raw edge (except shoulder seam), starting at top, proceeding down side, across bottom, and up other side to shoulder edge (following method used in step 8). Add lace as in step 8. Place overlay in exact position on top of side front/side back and baste in place. Handstitch in place. Repeat for other side front/side back overlay. With right sides together, sew shoulder seams, including all parts at one time.

10. Fit cuff piping to top edge of

sleeve cuff. Follow directions in step 8 for piping and add lace to top edge of sleeve cuff. With right sides together, sew side seam of sleeve cuff. Repeat for other sleeve cuff.

11. With right sides together, sew sleeve underarm seam. Press open. With sleeve remaining on wrong side, matching raw bottom edges and side seam of cuff with underarm seam of sleeve, place cuff on top of sleeve with right side of cuff against wrong side of sleeve. Handstitch seam at bottom edge. Turn sleeve, then cuff, to right side, bending cuff in place atop sleeve. Repeat for other cuff and sleeve.

12. With wrong side of dress facing you and the sleeve turned to the right side, matching sleeve top notch to shoulder seam, ease sleeve in place, pinning for smooth fit. Handstitch in place. Repeat for other sleeve.

13. Fit collar piping to edge (but not neckline) of collar. To pipe, follow directions in step 8, but omit lace along piping. With raw edge of piping matching raw edge of collar (except at neckline), pipe collar edge. With right sides together, sew collar lining to collar, except at neckline. Trim; clip curves; turn; press. Place raw edge of collar against neckline right sides up and matching center backs. Baste in place. Cut bias strip 5/8" wide and slightly longer than neckline. With right sides together, place bias strip at neckline. Sew all parts in place at one time. Trim seam. Turn bias strip to wrong side. Handstitch bias hem in place. Add lace at neckline.

14. Turn under front facings and handstitch in place.

15. Sew hooks and eyes to center-front opening. Sew tiny buttons down center-front.

16. Cut a length of both stiffening and lace, long enough to form knife pleats that fit under pleated section at back of dress. Place lace atop stiffening and form knife pleats. Press and baste in place. Fit under pleated section of dress (right sides of all parts facing out). Handstitch in place.

17. Optional: place large bow at center back.

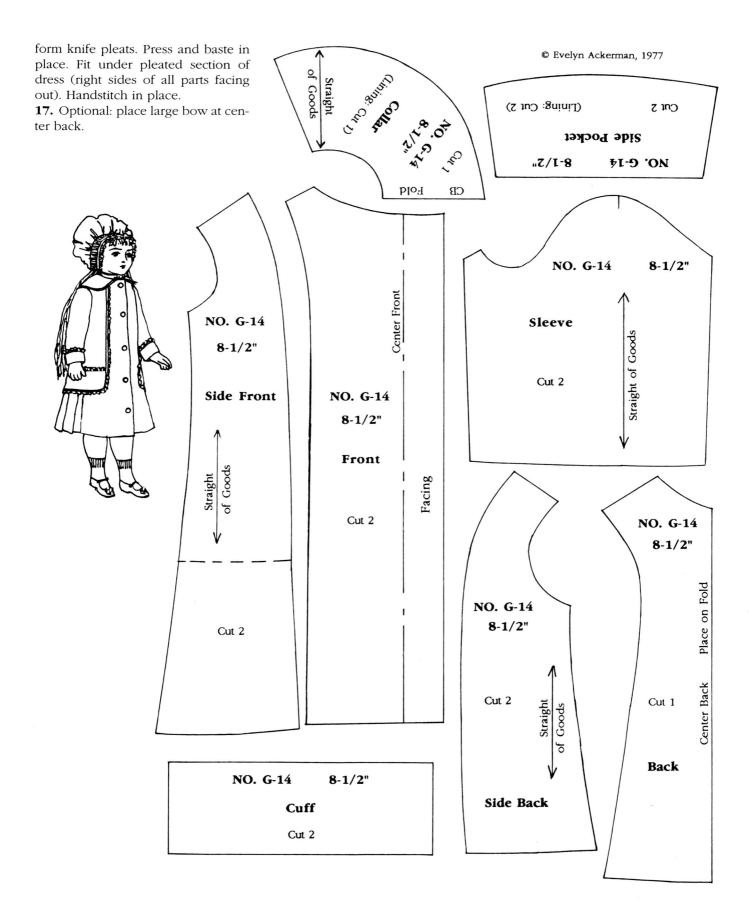

Collar

NO. G-14
8-1/2"

(Lining: Cut 1)

Cut 1

Straight of Goods

Fold

CB

Cut 2

Side Pocket

(Lining: Cut 2)

NO. G-14   8-1/2"

NO. G-14
8-1/2"

Side Front

Straight of Goods

Cut 2

NO. G-14
8-1/2"

Front

Center Front

Facing

Cut 2

NO. G-14   8-1/2"

Sleeve

Cut 2

Straight of Goods

NO. G-14
8-1/2"

Cut 2

Side Back

Straight of Goods

NO. G-14
8-1/2"

Cut 1

Center Back   Place on Fold

Back

NO. G-14   8-1/2"

Cuff

Cut 2

41

PART II

French, German and American Boy Dolls

PATTERN NO. B-15
FOR A 10 INCH BOY DOLL'S SUIT

General Instructions

- All pattern parts include 3/16" seams and hems, unless otherwise noted.
- Press all seams and hems as work proceeds.
- A very lightweight wool, flat-textured, in a solid color, such as navy blue, is most suitable, but a tightly woven, smooth-textured white cotton or a linen also could be used. The only trim is very narrow cotton or linen tape (white or beige, for dark color; navy blue for others).

Jacket

1. With right sides together, sew shoulder seams of jacket fronts and jacket back.

2. With right sides together, sew side seams.

3. Except at neckline, turn under all edges of collar. Handstitch in place. Baste two or three rows of narrow tape alongside hemmed edge of collar, about 1/16" apart. Handstitch in place. Place collar against neckline, right sides up, matching center backs, with front tips of collar at jacket front dots (see pattern). Baste in place. Cut bias strip 5/8" wide and slightly longer than collar neckline, using a lightweight cotton approximately the same color as jacket fabric. With right sides together, place bias strip at neckline. Baste, then sew in place. Turn bias to wrong side; press. Turn in bias ends and turn under bias hem. Handstitch hem on wrong side.

4. For sleeve cuff, cut rectangle of jacket fabric 2-1/4" wide x 3-1/2" long.

5. Sew tiny running stitches close to bottom edge of sleeve. With right sides together, sew sleeve underarm seam. With wrong sides together, fold sleeve cuff in half. Sew one or two pieces of

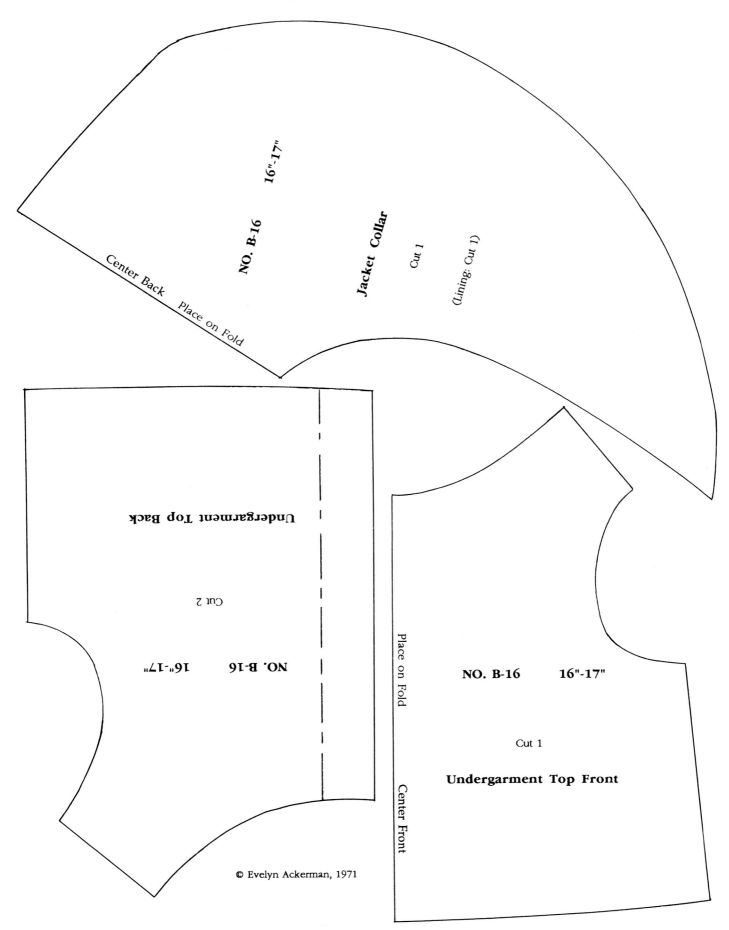

NO. B-16   16"-17"

Jacket Collar

Cut 1

(Lining: Cut 1)

Center Back   Place on Fold

Undergarment Top Back

Cut 2

NO. B-16   **16"-17"**

Place on Fold

Center Front

NO. B-16   16"-17"

Cut 1

Undergarment Top Front

© Evelyn Ackerman, 1971

49

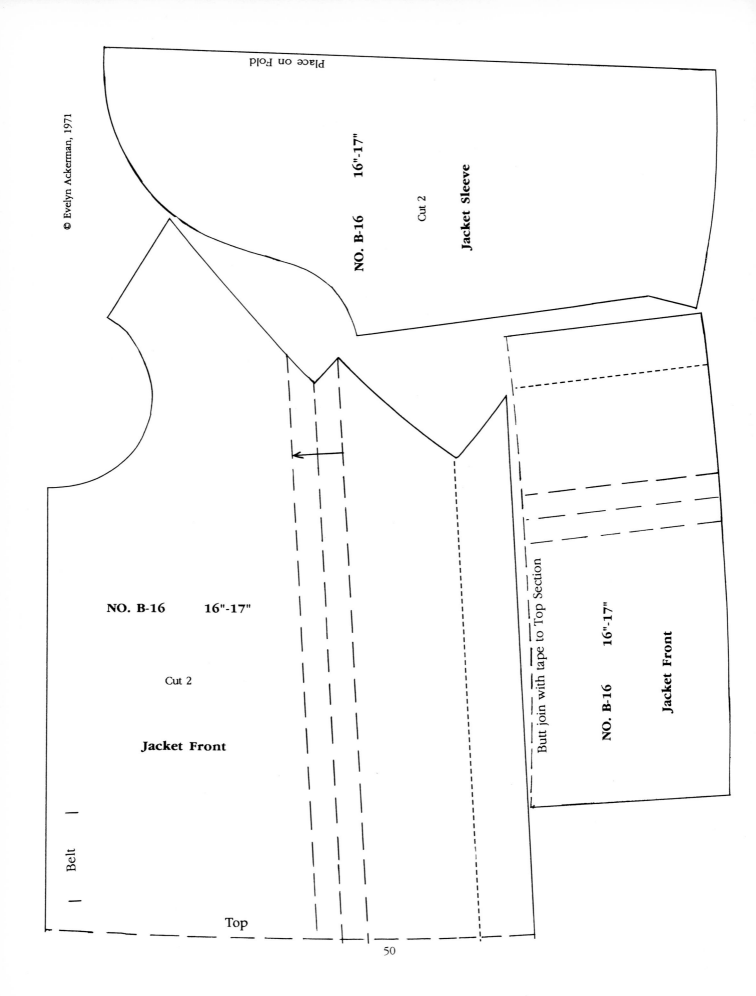

© Evelyn Ackerman, 1971

Place on Fold

NO. B-16   16"-17"

Cut 2

Jacket Sleeve

NO. B-16   16"-17"

Cut 2

Jacket Front

Belt

Top

Butt join with tape to Top Section

NO. B-16   16"-17"

Jacket Front

PATTERN NO. B-17
FOR A 12 TO 13 INCH BOY DOLL'S SUIT

General Instructions
- All pattern parts include 1/4" seams and hems, unless otherwise noted.
- Press all seams and hems as work proceeds.
- Cotton is the most suitable fabric, with the main sections made from a solid color or stripe and the neckband, cuff, leg band and belt made from white.

Jacket
1. With right sides together, sew shoulder seams, easing in fullness.
2. With right sides together, sew side seams.
3. With right sides together, sew shoulder seams of neckband.
4. With right sides up, baste neckband in place at raw neckline, matching shoulder seams.
5. Cut bias strip 5/8" wide and long enough to fit neckline. With right sides together, pin bias strip at neckline, matching raw edges. Baste, then sew in place. Trim and clip curves. Turn bias strip to wrong side and handstitch hem in place.
6. Turn under bottom hem of neckband. Press. Topstitch in place.
7. Cut rectangle 2" wide by 5-3/4" long from same fabric as neckband. With right sides together, sew to left center-front opening, along dotted line as per pattern part, allowing for 1/4" at top. Trim and press. Turn under 1/4" hem on raw edge and press in place. Bend in half to form center-front opening trim (turn under top raw edge). Handstitch everything in place.
8. Turn under hem facing on right side of center-front opening and sew in place.
9. For sleeve cuff, cut two rectangles 1-1/2" wide and long enough to fit over doll's hand easily and with 1/4" allowance for each side seam. Sew tiny running stitches to sleeve bottom raw edge. Gather to fit cuff. With right sides together, sew cuff to sleeve bottom. Turn under 1/8" hem on cuff bottom and press in place. On wrong side, handstitch cuff to sleeve bottom seam. Press cuff seam and bottom edge. Repeat for other cuff.
10. Sew tiny running stitches at sleeve cap. With right sides together, sew sleeve underarm seam, including cuff. With wrong side of jacket facing you and sleeve turned to right side, put sleeve into armhole, matching underarm seam to side seam and center top of sleeve to shoulder seam. Pin, easing the cap in place by adjusting gathering stitches (will ease into a smooth fitting cap). Sew sleeve in place. Trim seam. Repeat for other sleeve.
11. Turn under jacket bottom hem. Handstitch in place.
12. On center-front opening trim (left side), sew four evenly spaced buttonholes, beginning at top. On right side, sew four buttons.
13. For belt, cut rectangle 1-3/4" wide x 13-1/4" long. With right sides together, sew seam along both long edges and one short side edge. Turn belt to right side and press. Turn under seams of open end and handstitch in place. Overlap belt in crossed position, mark position for snap and sew it in place at center.

Pants
1. Form box pleats, as indicated on pattern. Sew in place across top edge.
2. With right sides together, sew center-front seam from top to dot. Repeat for center-back seam.
3. With right sides together, sew left side seam from notch to bottom. Press open, including side opening hems to form placket. Sew in place.
4. With right sides together, sew right side seam.

Photograph: Bob Lopez

5. Sew machine gathering stitches along bottom leg edges. Cut two bias strips 1" wide x 5" long. With right sides together, fit gathered leg bottom to bias strip. Sew in place. Trim seam and press. Turn bias strip to wrong side, forming narrow leg band. Sew bias strip hem on wrong side.
6. With right sides together, matching center-front seam to center-back seam, sew inside pants legs from bottom of one leg band, around curve, to bottom of other leg band. Reinforce seam stitching at crotch. Clip curves.
7. For waistband, cut rectangle 1" wide x 9-1/2" long. With right sides together, sew waistband to pants at waist, allowing extension on one side at opening. Press and turn to wrong side, forming waistband. Turn under long waistband hem and sew on wrong side, including extension and raw ends.
8. Sew snaps to waistband to close.

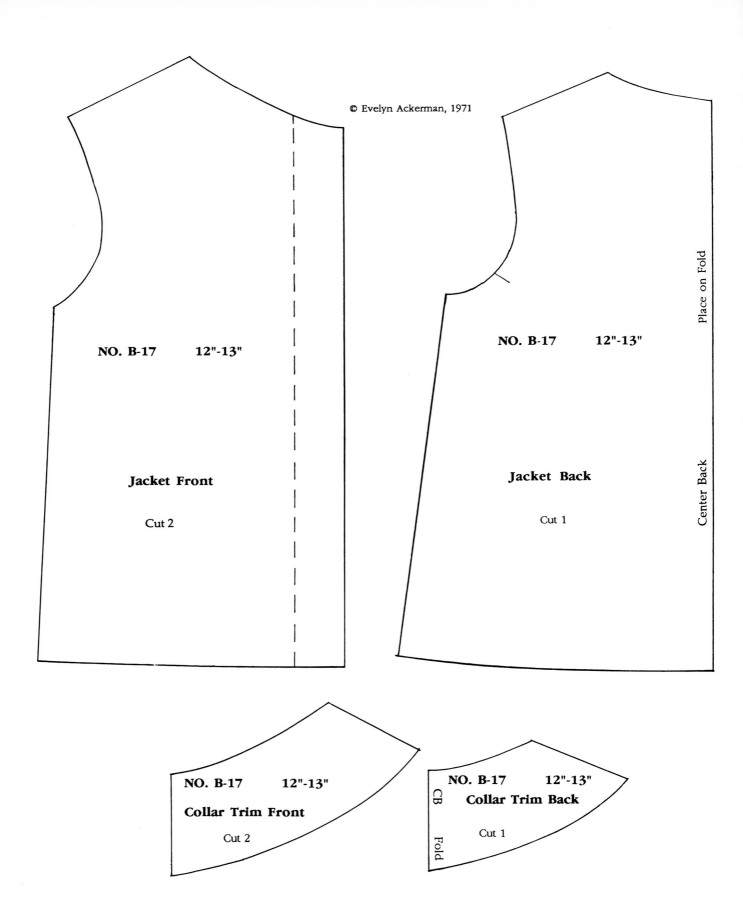

© Evelyn Ackerman, 1971

Place on Fold

Center Back

NO. B-17   12"-13"

Jacket Front

Cut 2

NO. B-17   12"-13"

Jacket Back

Cut 1

NO. B-17   12"-13"

Collar Trim Front

Cut 2

NO. B-17   12"-13"

Collar Trim Back

Cut 1

CB

Fold

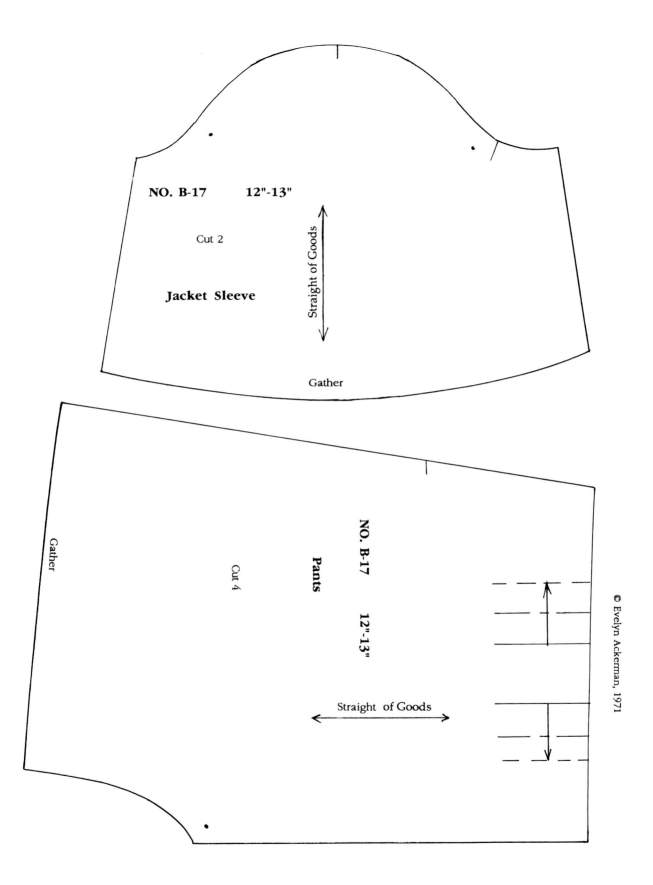

NO. B-17   12"-13"

Cut 2

Jacket Sleeve

Straight of Goods

Gather

Gather

Cut 4

NO. B-17

Pants

12"-13"

Straight of Goods

© Evelyn Ackerman, 1971

53

PATTERN NO. S-33
FOR A 16 TO 17 INCH BOY DOLL'S SUIT

General Instructions

- All pattern parts include 1/4" seams and hems, unless otherwise noted.
- Press all seams and hems as work proceeds.
- A lightly starched cotton with a tight weave is most suitable. Solid colors (such as pale blue with white dickey) are best. However, patterned cottons, such as stripes, checks or plaids, are also attractive choices.

Jacket

1. With right sides together, sew shoulder seams.

2. With right sides together, sew side seams.

3. Pleat sleeve bottom towards center (three pleats each side of center). Sew pleats in place, up one side to horizontal dotted line, as per pattern, across, and down other side. Press pleats to top of sleeve cap (or baste in place). Repeat for other sleeve.

4. Cut rectangle 7/8" wide by the length of finished sleeve bottom. With right sides together, place fabric rectangle against sleeve bottom, matching raw edges. Sew in place. Turn rectangle to wrong side and press, forming sleeve hem. Sew hem in place. Repeat for other sleeve.

5. With right sides together, sew sleeve underarm seam. With wrong side of jacket facing you and sleeve turned to right side, matching center of sleeve cap to shoulder seam and sleeve underarm seam to side seam, ease sleeve into place with pins. Adjust to fit. Sew sleeve in place. Repeat for other sleeve.

6. With right sides together, sew collar to collar lining, leaving raw neckline open. Trim seam and corners; turn and press. Topstitch in place along all edges except raw neckline.

7. With right sides up, baste collar at raw neckline opening, matching at the center backs.

8. As per pattern, cut across top dotted line for right front opening. Turn under raw top edge (alongside collar), and then turn hem under long front edge, forming extended front right side opening (underlap for buttons). Sew in place. Press.

9. Turn under hem of left side front opening, flush with collar edge. Sew in place.

10. Cut bias strip 3/4" wide x 10-3/4" long. With right sides together, baste bias strip to raw neckline opening, including extension of right front opening and turning under raw side edges. Sew in place. Trim seam and clip curves. Turn to wrong side and sew bias strip hem in place.

11. Pin jacket's bottom hem in place, leaving front sides open. Insert elastic and pin hem. Sew bottom hem in place without catching elastic into stitching. Fit to doll and pull elastic for desired tension and position. Tack elastic firmly in place.

12. Sew three buttons to right front opening and three buttonholes to left front opening.

Pants

1. With right sides together, sew center-front seam.

2. With right sides together, sew center-back seam.

3. Turn under bottom pant leg hem and sew in place. Repeat for other pant leg.

4. With right sides together, matching center-front seams and center-back seams, sew pant legs together, from bottom, around curve, to other bottom. Clip curve.

5. Slash sides from top to dot for side plackets. Bind and hem (front of pants overlaps back): binding for front edge of placket will turn under flush at seam and be stitched in place, while binding for back edge of placket will be sewn to edge of slash and extend beyond,

being placed under front placket edge; binding is all one piece.

6. With right sides together, sew front waistband to pant top, turning under 1/4" side hems. Turn at seam to wrong side, forming waistband. Press. Sew hem in place (1/2" finished width).

7. At placket openings, sew buttonholes on front and buttons on back.

Dickey

1. Sew hem on all edges, except neckline.

2. Cut rectangle 3/4" wide x 7" long for neckband. With right sides together, baste to neckline (1/8" seam). Sew in place. Bend approximately in half, to form neckband, but allow for hem on wrong side. Topstitch in place along all edges of neckband.

3. Sew button and buttonhole at neckband back opening.

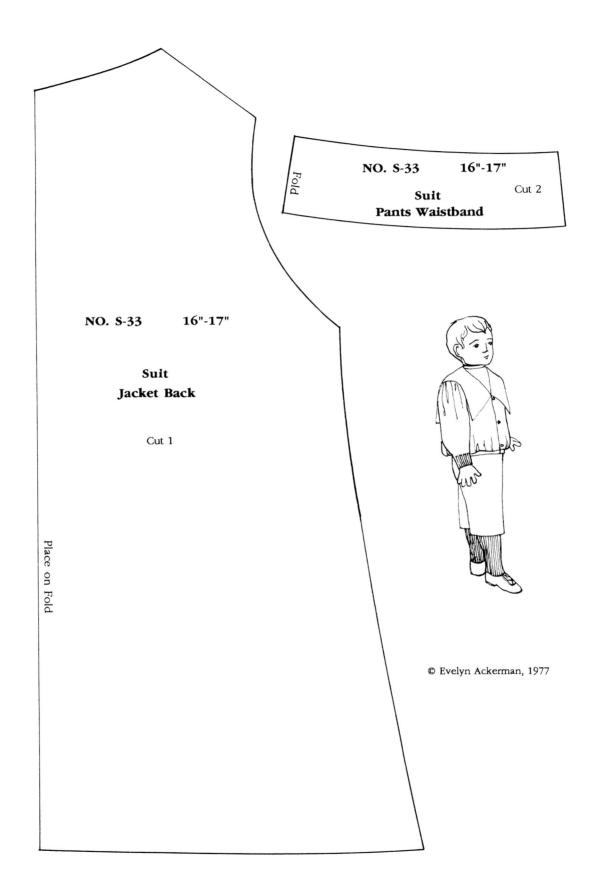

NO. S-33   **16"-17"**

Fold

Suit
Pants Waistband

Cut 2

NO. S-33   **16"-17"**

Suit
Jacket Back

Cut 1

Place on Fold

© Evelyn Ackerman, 1977

55

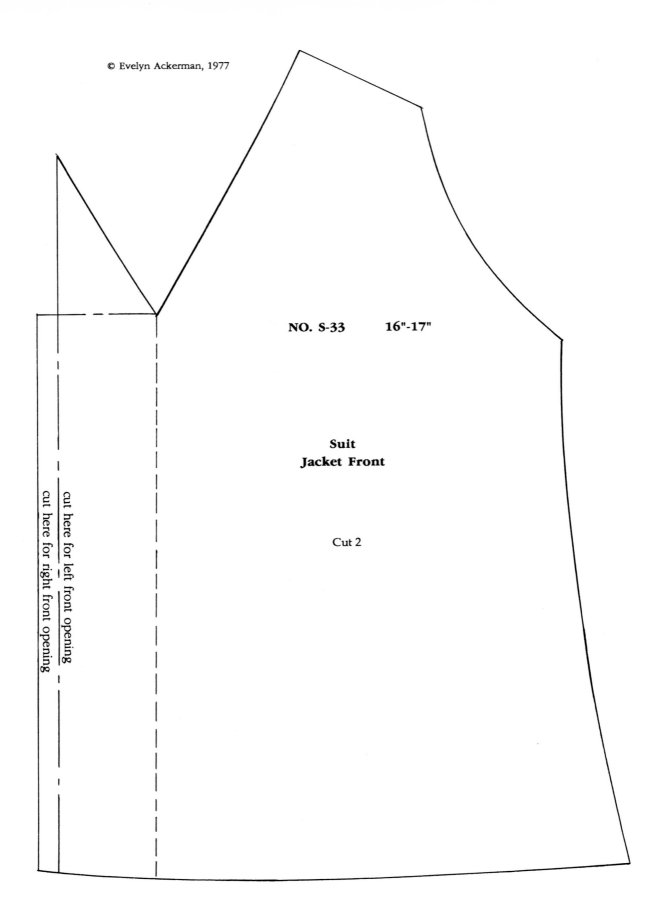

NO. S-33   16"-17"

**Suit
Jacket Front**

Cut 2

cut here for left front opening

cut here for right front opening

PATTERN NO. F-19
FOR A 12-1/2 INCH FASHION DOLL'S DRESS

General Instructions

- All pattern parts include 1/8" seams and hems, unless otherwise noted.
- Press all seams and hems as work proceeds.
- Representing a two-piece summer gown (a fashionable adaptation of an 1860s adult garment), it is appropriately made from white piqué. Piqué was a popular choice for warm-weather clothing in the mid 19th century because it was both stiff enough not to require a lining, but sufficiently pliable to afford its wearer maximum comfort. The style, itself, is one that could have been worn in any season. Other suitable fabrics from which to make it are linen, plain silk, faille, taffeta or wool. When a lining is required, it should be made from the same pattern parts as the garment itself. The lining should be sewn as one with the garment.

Bodice Jacket

1. With right sides together, sew each front to each side.
2. With right sides together, easing in fullness, sew each side to each back from dot to top. With right sides together, sew each side to each back from bottom to x. On wrong side, pull each side of the open, horizontal section of pleat that is not sewn so it lies straight across center back. Tack in place at dot on each side seam (do not allow stitch to show on right side). Press along top 1/2" only of pleat. To hold in place permanently, at both dots tack narrow, 1/2" long piece of tape on wrong side of bodice jacket.
3. With right sides together, sew shoulder seams.
4. Fit unfinished bodice jacket to doll. Turn under front facings (as per dotted line on pattern). Handstitch facings in place.
5. Turn under narrow bottom hem. Press. Using cross stitch, sew raw edge firmly in place.

6. To form piping for sleeves, cut two 1/2" wide bias strips, at least 1/4" longer than sleeve opening. Place narrow cord (string) on wrong side of center of each bias strip and fold the bias strip in half, right sides out. Sew tiny running stitches as close to cord as possible along entire length of each bias strip Trim each so that remaining seam allowance is only 1/8".
7. Matching raw edges, place piping against right side of bodice jacket's sleeve armhole opening. Handstitch in place along original handstitching of piping. Repeat for other sleeve.
8. With right sides together, sew inside curve of upper sleeve to under sleeve. Turn under bottom sleeve hem and handstitch in place. Approximately 1/8" above sleeve bottom, handstitch narrow white braid from open seam edge to opposite open seam edge. With right sides together, sew outside curve of upper sleeve to under sleeve. Repeat for other sleeve.
9. With wrong side of bodice jacket facing you and the sleeve turned to

right side, matching long sleeve seam to front bodice notch, place sleeve into armhole opening and ease in fullness with pins for smooth fit. Handstitch in place against original stitching at piping cord. Repeat for other sleeve.
10. Sew narrow white braid to bodice jacket, beginning at neckline on one side and ending at neckline on other side, approximately 1/2" from front openings (allowing for buttons and buttonholes) and 1/8" from all other edges.
11. For neckband, cut straight length of jacket fabric 3/4" wide and 1/4" longer than neck opening. With right sides together, matching raw edge of 3/4" wide fabric length to raw edge of neck opening and allowing 1/8" extension on each side, sew neckband in place. Bend to inside, forming 1/4" wide neckband. Turn under hems and side edges on wrong side and handstitch in place.
12. On right side, as per pattern, cut and handstitch buttonholes. On left

65

side, sew buttons in place. At neck-band, sew tiny hook and eye.

Skirt

1. With right sides together, sew skirt front to skirt sides.

2. With right sides together, sew each skirt side to each skirt back.

3. With right sides together, sew center-back seam from bottom to dot. Press open. Turn under center-back opening from dot to top and hand-stitch in place.

4. Fit unfinished skirt on doll. Form one pleat on each back panel and one pleat on each side panel (closer to back than middle of panel) so that skirt fits doll at waist. Tack each pleat in place close to waistline.

5. For waistband, cut skirt fabric 3/4" wide and 1/4" longer than waistline opening. Matching raw edges, place right side of waistband against right side of skirt at waistline. Sew in place. Turn waistband to wrong side so that finished waistband is approximately 1/4" wide. Turn under inside hem and side edges and sew in place.

6. Sew hook and eye at center back of waistband.

7. Using any suitable lining fabric, cut a 1" wide bias strip that is 1/4" longer than bottom of skirt. With right sides together, sew bias strip to skirt bottom. Turn to wrong side so that no edge of bias strip shows on right side. Baste in place; press. Turn under raw edge and handstitch hem in place.

8. On right side, along hem's stitching, sew narrow white braid around entire width of skirt. About 1/8" below this, sew a second row of braid around entire width of skirt.

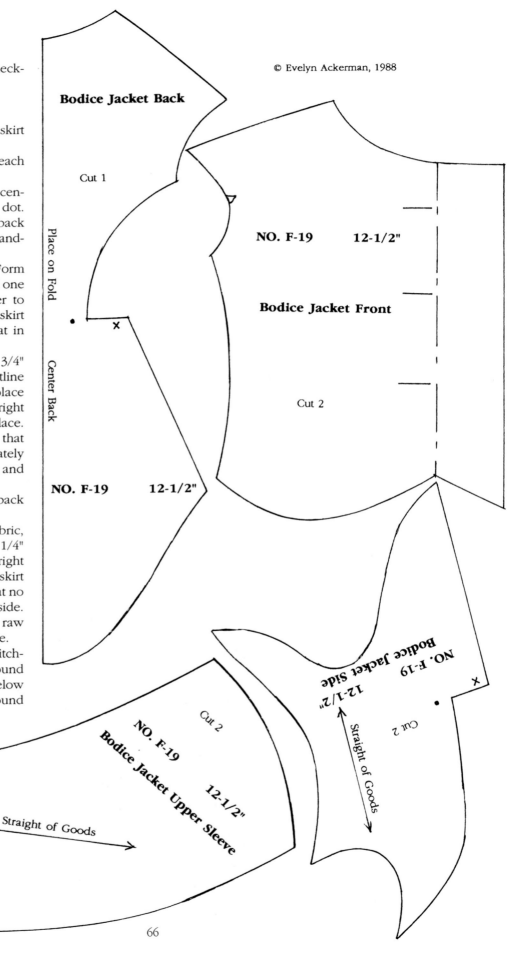

© Evelyn Ackerman, 1988

66

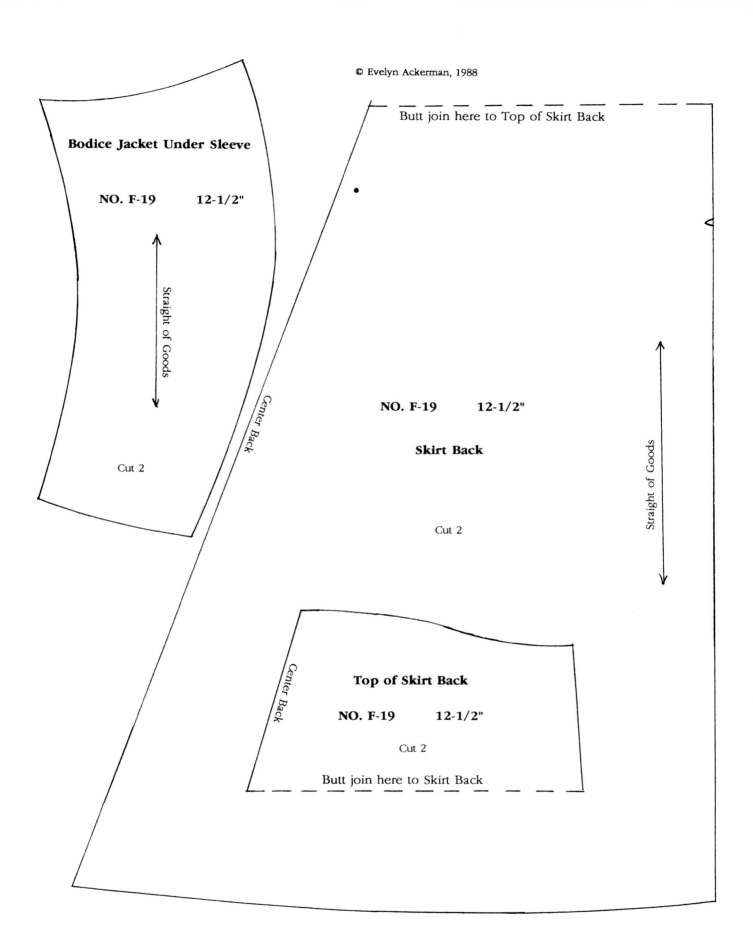

Bodice Jacket Under Sleeve

NO. F-19   **12-1/2"**

Straight of Goods

Center Back

Cut 2

Butt join here to Top of Skirt Back

NO. F-19   **12-1/2"**

Skirt Back

Cut 2

Straight of Goods

Top of Skirt Back

NO. F-19   **12-1/2"**

Cut 2

Center Back

Butt join here to Skirt Back

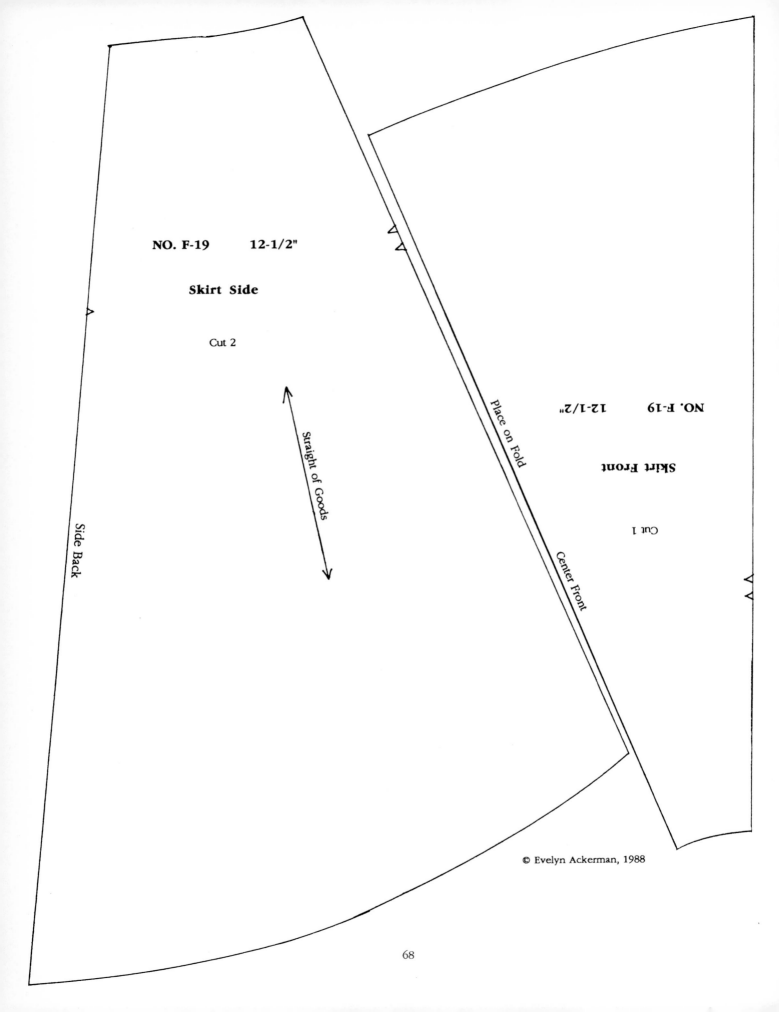

NO. F-19   12-1/2"

Skirt Side

Cut 2

Straight of Goods

Place on Fold

Center Front

Side Back

NO. F-19   12-1/2"

Skirt Front

Cut 1

© Evelyn Ackerman, 1988

PATTERN NO. F-21
FOR A 15 INCH FASHION DOLL'S DRESS

General Instructions
- All pattern parts include 1/8" seams and hems, unless otherwise noted.
- Press all seams and hems as work proceeds.
- Garment, as illustrated, is made from lightweight patterned wool, lined with lightweight linen and open-weave cotton. Two related laces, with open-work design and scalloped edge, approximately 1" wide and 1/4" wide are needed.

How to make bias strips that look like piping
1. Cut bias strip from garment fabric, approximately 1" wide and as long as parts to be falsely piped. If necessary, join more than one piece to achieve desired length.
2. Fold in half, right sides out. Press.
3. Place bias under hem of garment section to be "piped" and attach by using running stitch, leaving 3/32" of bias showing to simulate piping.

Jacket (sew as one with lining)
1. With right sides together, sew darts. Slit open to about 1/4" from point of dart.
2. With right sides together, sew center-back seam of back.
3. With right sides together, sew side to back.
4. With right sides together, sew side to front.
5. With right sides together, sew shoulder seams.
6. With right sides together, sew one seam of sleeve top to under sleeve. Hem sleeve bottom. Edge sleeve bottom with bias strip to simulate piping. Cut another bias strip 1-1/2" x 10". Fold in half and press. With some spacing between pleats, form box pleats. Place along sleeve bottom with raw edge underneath sleeve and extension of pleats beyond sleeve bottom about 1/4". Handstitch in place. Next,

handstitch lace to sleeve bottom so that it extends another 1/4" below box pleats. With right sides together, sew other sleeve seam (top sleeve to under sleeve). Repeat for other sleeve.

7. With wrong side of jacket facing you and sleeve turned to the right side, fit sleeve into armhole, matching center-top of sleeve cap to shoulder seam. Ease in fullness, pinning in place for smooth fit. Sew in place. Repeat for other sleeve.

8. Turn under neckline hem. Sew in place. Place bias strip along neckline to simulate piping (same as for sleeve). Sew in place.

9. Turn under bottom hem of jacket. Sew in place. Place bias strip along jacket bottom to simulate piping (same as for sleeve). Sew in place.

10. Fit jacket to doll and turn under center-front facings, allowing for enough overlap to accommodate buttons and buttonholes (or buttons and hooks and eyes) Sew in place.

11. Sew lace along bottom edge of jacket, with about 1/2" extension.

12. Sew lace (about 1/4" wide) at neckline, matching flat edge of lace to top edge of bias false piping, turning raw lace ends to inside of jacket at center front. Sew in place. Using same lace, place along underside of neckline bias false piping and loosely pleat to give some fullness, with about 1/4" of lace extending above bias. Sew in place.

13. At center front, sew buttons and buttonholes (or buttons and hooks and eyes).

Skirt

1. Baste side front top (both Section A and Section B) to side front top lining (wrong sides facing each other, placed to match shaded areas on pattern part).

2. With right sides together, sew side front bottom to side front top lining.

3. With right sides together, sew side front to back.

4. With right sides together, sew front top lining and front bottom (slightly overlapping along horizontal raw edge) to side front..

5. Slash center-back opening from top to dot. Turn under center-back opening hems and sew in place. At bottom of center-back opening, form one pleat and tack in place (this acts as placket).

6. With right sides together, matching notches, sew back overlap facing to back overlay. Turn and press. Fold, as per dotted line on pattern, towards center-back. Press. Turn under bottom edge and center-back edge to form hems and handstitch to lining. Matching top waistline raw edges, place each separate back overlay on skirt back (long straight hemmed edge matching center-back seam). Pin in place. Handstitch right and left back overlays together (overlap one on other very slightly) between large dots. Using small running stitch, attach upper portion only of long raw edge (overlapping about 1/8") at side-back seam. At waistline, form three knife pleats (facing center-back on each side), with first pleat at edge of center-back opening. Baste in place about 3" from top. At top, sew across raw waistline edge, fixing pleats at this point permanently. About 1" below center-back opening, backstitch across all pleating in straight line. Press pleats. Remove basting. Tack lace to overlay panel, starting at point where front overlay panel's bottom will meet back overlay panel, proceeding to bottom of panel, across bottom, up along center back and down opposite panel, ending at same place on opposite side. The lace must be placed so that it is underneath the panel, extending about 1/2" below, including the folded triangular section (where it is in reversed position in order to achieve a continuous appearance).

7. Place bow with large, flat, center knot at center back, with bow centered over backstitched part of back overlay panel.

8. Baste front overlay to front overlay lining. Form two pleats, as per pattern, shaped horizontally and at a slight downward diagonal towards center. Baste and press in place. At center front it will be necessary to tack

these down, giving the appearance of a center-front seam. Turn under hem along all edges, except top, and handstitch in place. Except at top, edge with bias strip to simulate piping. Edge bottom length (not sides or top) with lace. Pin panel in position on front of skirt so that sides overlap side seams about 1/8", covering raw edge of back overlay, and matching top raw edges. Baste in place along top raw edge. Handstitch in place at side seam, using hidden stitches. At center front of horizontal pleats, tack flat knotted ribbon in place.

9. Sew 1-1/2" wide false hem (can be made from bias strip, if wish) to entire length of bottom. Turn, press and baste in place. Optional: on wrong side, add stiffened, pleated, lace-edged trim at hemline, about 1-1/2" wide and as long as hem.

10. Cut (and piece together) bias strip approximately 2-1/2" wide x 70" long. Fold in half, right sides out, and press. Make box pleats entire length, with pleats approximately 3/8" wide and with 1/8" space between pleats. Baste and press in place. Place against skirt so that bottom of pleats match bottom of hem. Stitch across top near raw edge. Repeat another strip of box pleating and place on dress above bottom row of pleating, so that this overlaps bottom row about 1/4" (must cover raw top edge of bottom row of pleating). Make a bias tape from dress fabric (about 5/8" wide so that when each long side is turned under, the finished size will be about 1/4" wide), long enough to cover raw edge of top row of pleating. Handstitch in place.

11. Repeat another two short rows (approximately seven pleats wide) of box pleating, made as above. Place between seams of sides, with bottom of pleating just touching top of bias trim on top of long row of pleating. Cover raw top edge of short rows of pleating with bias tape, too.

12. Cut waistband from lining fabric, approximately 1" wide x 8" long (fit to doll). Sew in place. Secure waistband with hook and eye.

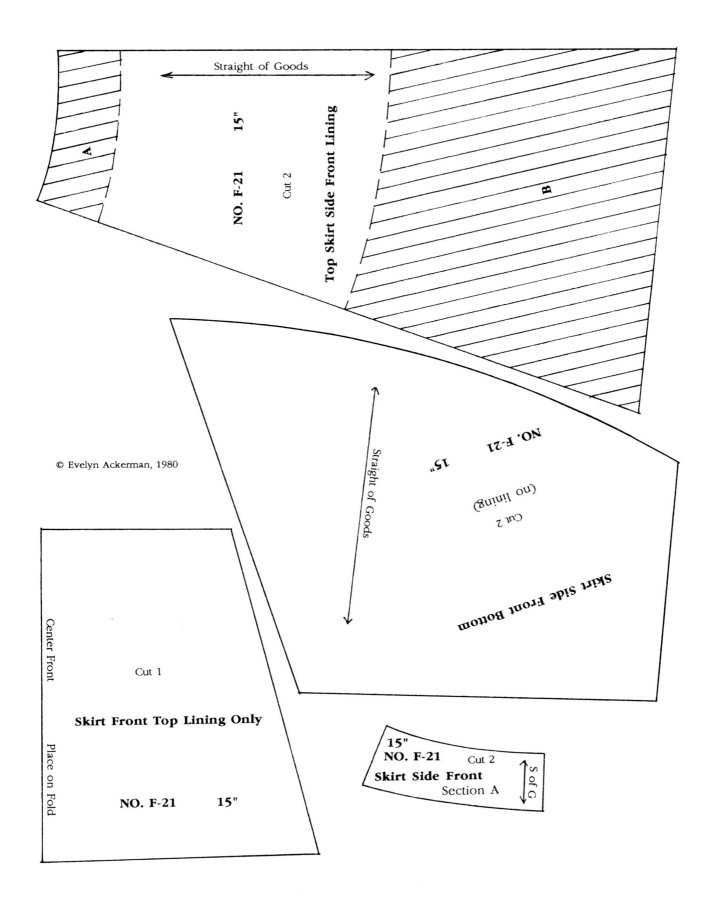

Straight of Goods

A

NO. F-21   15"

Cut 2

Top Skirt Side Front Lining

B

© Evelyn Ackerman, 1980

Straight of Goods

NO. F-21

15"

Cut 2
(no lining)

Skirt Side Front Bottom

Center Front

Cut 1

Skirt Front Top Lining Only

NO. F-21   15"

Place on Fold

15"
NO. F-21   Cut 2
Skirt Side Front
Section A

S of G

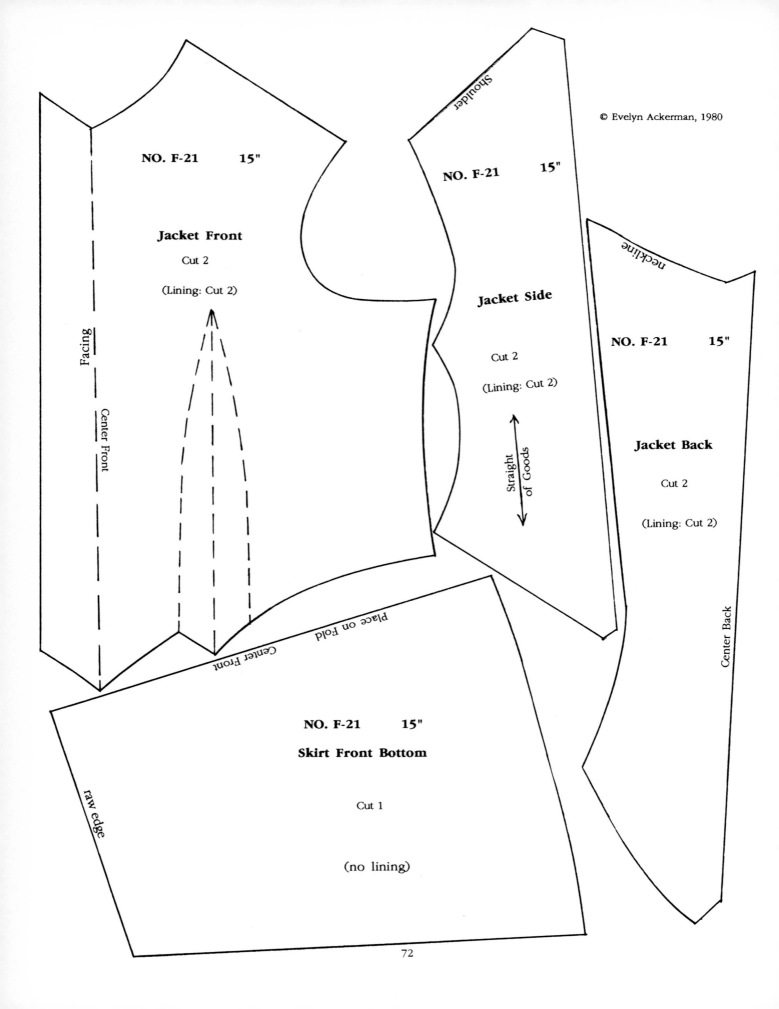

NO. F-21   15"

Jacket Front

Cut 2

(Lining: Cut 2)

Facing

Center Front

Shoulder

NO. F-21   15"

© Evelyn Ackerman, 1980

Jacket Side

Cut 2

(Lining: Cut 2)

Straight of Goods

neckline

NO. F-21   15"

Jacket Back

Cut 2

(Lining: Cut 2)

Center Back

place on Fold   Center Front

NO. F-21   15"

Skirt Front Bottom

Cut 1

(no lining)

raw edge

72

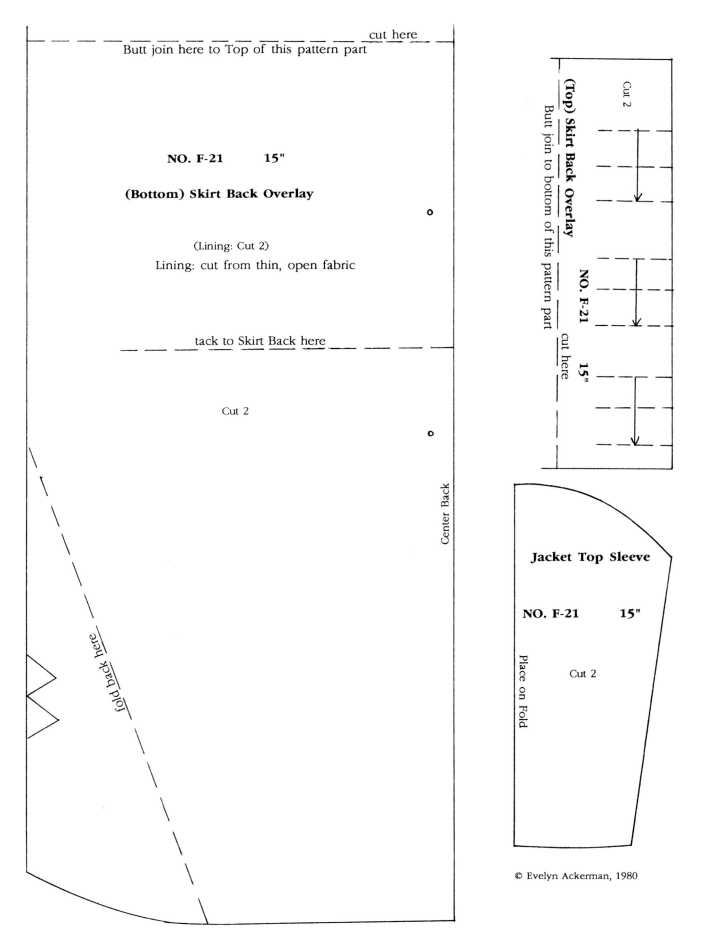

cut here

Butt join here to Top of this pattern part

NO. F-21   15"

(Bottom) Skirt Back Overlay

(Lining: Cut 2)

Lining: cut from thin, open fabric

tack to Skirt Back here

Cut 2

o

o

Center Back

fold back here

(Top) Skirt Back Overlay

Butt join to bottom of this pattern part

Cut 2

NO. F-21   15"

cut here

Jacket Top Sleeve

NO. F-21   15"

Cut 2

Place on Fold

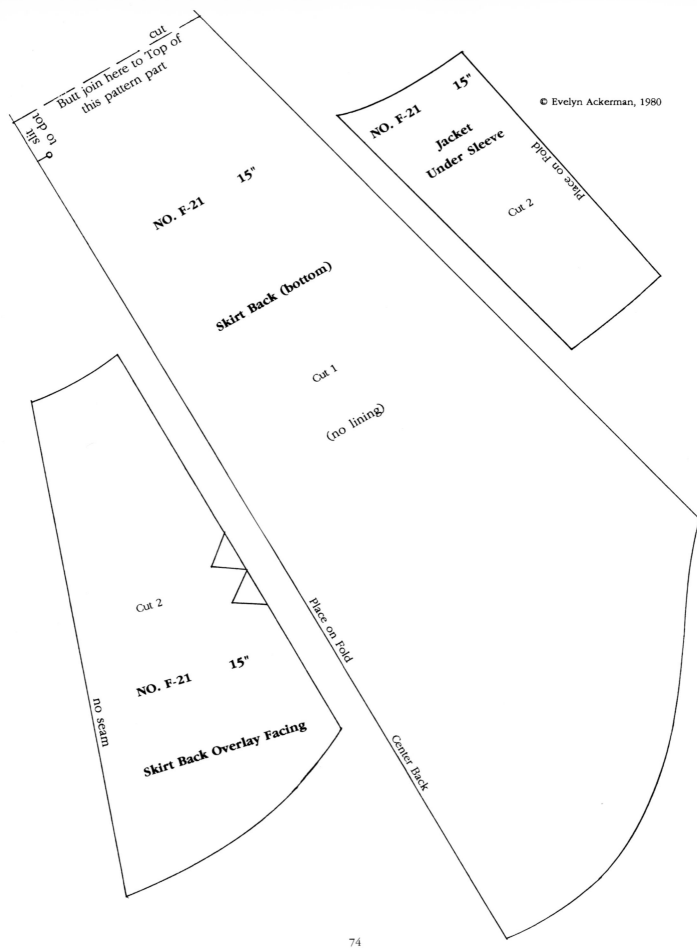

Butt join here to Top of
this pattern part

cut

slit
to dot

NO. F-21   15"

Skirt Back (bottom)

Cut 1

(no lining)

NO. F-21   15"

Jacket
Under Sleeve

Cut 2

place on fold

© Evelyn Ackerman, 1980

Place on Fold

Center Back

Cut 2

no seam

NO. F-21   15"

Skirt Back Overlay Facing

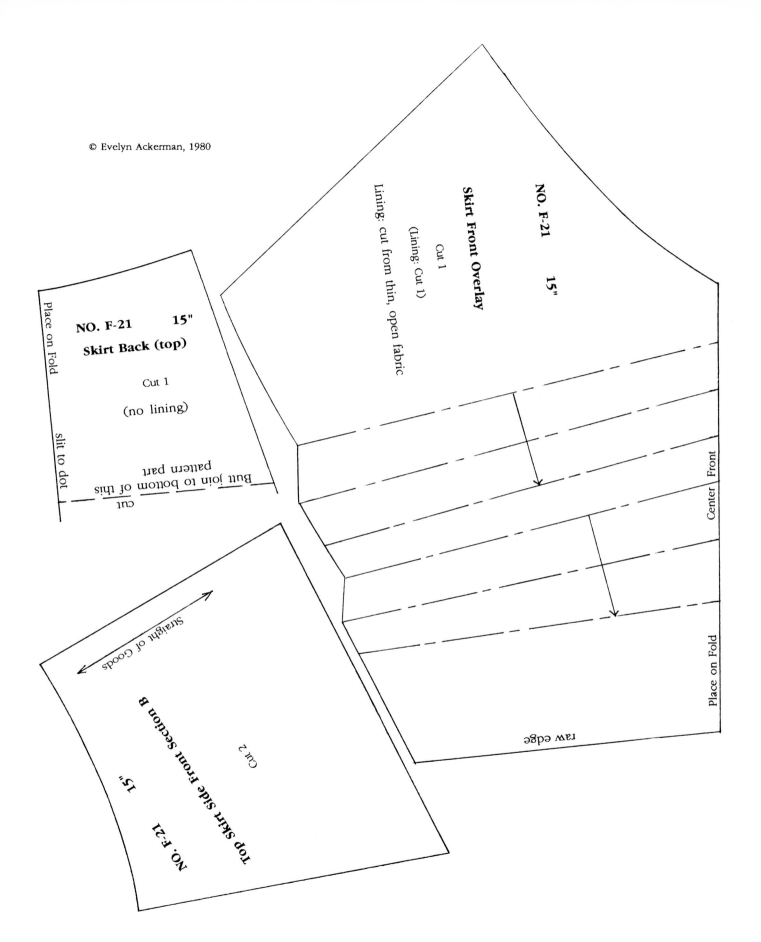

NO. F-21   15"

Skirt Front Overlay

Cut 1

(Lining: Cut 1)

Lining: cut from thin, open fabric

Center Front

Place on Fold

raw edge

NO. F-21   15"

Skirt Back (top)

Cut 1

(no lining)

Place on Fold

slit to dot

cut

Butt join to bottom of this pattern part

Straight of Goods

NO. F-21   15"

Top Skirt Side Front Section B

Cut 2

PATTERN NO. F-22
FOR A 15 INCH FASHION DOLL'S DRESS AND TOQUE

General Instructions

• All pattern parts include 3/16" seams and hems, unless otherwise noted.

• Press all seams and hems as work proceeds.

• If necessary, piece fabric to make bias strips long enough to fit appropriate parts.

• Sew lining as one with jacket.

• Sometimes a more professional appearance can be achieved if a seamline is basted before final sewing, especially at neckline curves and similar areas.

• Using contrasting fabric colors, such as black and tan, gray and plum or brown and beige, select suitable fabrics, such as lightweight wool, faille, velvet or medium weight silk, to make this two-piece dress.

Jacket

1. With right sides together, sew backs at center-back seam.

2. With right sides together, easing in fullness, sew side backs to back.

3. With right sides together, sew side backs to side fronts.

4. Sew basting line about 1/2" from waistline edge across bottom of jacket. With right sides together, place one long raw edge of waistband against basting across bottom of jacket and with other raw edge toward top of jacket. Sew in place from large dot to large dot. Pin in place away from other parts to be sewn to avoid it being caught into other seams.

5. Cut two bias strips (contrasting color) 3/4" wide x 7" long. Bend in half, right sides out, and press. With right sides together, matching raw edges and beginning at neckline, baste bias strip to front seam of side front from neckline to +. Press. Turn dangling extension of bias strip at bottom edge across bottom edge of front, with raw edges matching. Baste in place.

6. With right sides together, sew shoulder seams.

7. With right sides together, sew under sleeve to upper sleeve at long seam. With right sides together, sew matching seam of cuff. Cut bias strip (contrasting color), as long as upper edge of cuff and 3/4" wide. Bend in half, right sides out, and press. With right sides together, matching top raw edges, sew bias to cuff. Press so that bias forms finished edge at top of cuff. With right sides together, sew other sleeve seam. With right sides together, sew other cuff seam. With right side of cuff facing wrong side of sleeve bottom, matching raw bottom edges and seams, sew cuff to sleeve. Turn sleeve and cuff to right side and press. Repeat for other sleeve.

8. With wrong side of jacket facing you and sleeve turned to right side, matching sleeve notch at cap to shoulder seam, put sleeve into armhole. Ease in fullness and pin in place for smooth fit. Sew in place. Repeat for other sleeve.

9. Cut bias strip (contrasting color) length of neckline and 5/8" wide. Bend in half, right sides out. With right sides together, place bias strip at neckline, matching raw edges. Sew in place. Press with finished edge up and raw edge of bias turned to wrong side. Handstitch bias hem on wrong side.

10. Fit jacket to doll and turn under front facings (see pattern dotted line), with jacket overlap sufficient to allow for buttons and buttonholes. Handstitch in place.

11. With right sides together, sew center-back seam of peplum backs.

12. With right sides together, sew peplum side backs to peplum back.

13. With right sides together, sew peplum fronts to peplum side backs.

14. Cut bias strip 3/4" wide (contrasting color) and long enough to encase entire scalloped bottom edge. With right sides together, place bias against scalloped edge of peplum, matching raw edges, and allow 1/4"+ to extend beyond dot at front scallops. Sew in place, following curves of each scallop. Trim seams and clip curves. Turn to wrong side and sew raw edges to jacket lining of peplum.

15. With right sides together, place revers (lapel; contrasting color) against front of peplum. Sew in place from top notch to notch at bottom by scallop. Trim seam. Turn to right side and press. Bend revers back onto peplum, as per dotted line. Press in place. Tack at waist seam.

16. With right sides together, matching seams and center fronts, sew peplum to jacket at waist, being careful not to catch in waistband. If possible, layer cut underneath part of waistline seam to eliminate some of bulk. Press down and handstitch in place (do not allow stitching to show on right side).

17. Tack raw sides of waistband under bias edge of front. Turn under bottom hem of waistband so that waistband just covers waistline seam. Sew in place.

18. Sew buttons and buttonholes on center-front opening.

Skirt

1. With right sides together, sew front to sides.

2. With right sides together, sew sides to backs.

3. With right sides together, sew center-back seam from bottom to dot.

4. Turn under hems and handstitch skirt center-back opening to skirt lining center-back opening.

5. Cut bias strip (contrasting color) 3/4" wide and long enough to fit bottom edge of skirt. Matching one long raw edge of bias to bottom raw

edge of skirt, with right sides together, sew bias in place. Turn bias to wrong side and handstitch to skirt lining.

6. For skirt ruffle, cut bias strip (skirt color), 2" wide x 50" long. With right sides together, sew center-back seam. Cut two bias strips (contrasting color) 3/4" wide x 50" long. Bend bias strips in half, right sides out. With right sides together, matching raw edges, sew each bias strip to each long edge of skirt ruffle. Turn raw edges to wrong side. Press. Cut skirt ruffle lining (bias) 2" wide x 50" long. Bend under hems along both long edges and handstitch skirt ruffle lining to skirt ruffle on wrong side. Press. About 1/2" from one long edge of skirt ruffle, sew running stitch. With right sides up, place skirt ruffle about 3/4" above bottom of skirt and gather to fit. Sew in place, stitching over running stitches.

7. For waistband, cut a straight of goods rectangle (skirt fabric) about 1" wide and slightly longer than doll's waist. With right sides together, matching one long raw edge to skirt waist, extending side ends of waistband slightly beyond center-back opening, and tuck pleating skirt backs to fit waistband, sew in place. Press. Bend in half to wrong side. On wrong side, turn under hem and raw side ends and sew in place.

8. Sew hook and eye at center back of waistband.

Toque

1. For headband (skirt fabric), cut bias strip 1-1/4" wide x 6-3/4" long. Repeat for inner lining (cloth that is a slight stiffener) and lining.

2. With right sides together, sew one long seam of headband to headband lining. Turn to right side and press.

3. Trim away top and bottom long seams from inner lining. Place against wrong side of fabric and baste in place.

4. Release headband lining so hangs free and turn under hem on top long edge of headband.

5. Fit headband to doll's head. With right sides together, sew center-back seam.

6. Fit crown to headband, gathering between dots to fit. Matching centers, place crown under pressed hem of headband, all right sides facing out. Do not include lining. Pin in place so crown is flat at back and slightly poofed between dots (front). Handstitch in place.

7. On wrong side, turn under headband lining hem and handstitch in place.

8. For headband overlay tie, cut straight of goods rectangle (contrasting fabric) about 1" wide and about double length of headband. With right sides together, sew long seam (with opening for turning). Turn to right side and handstitch opening. Press. Place against headband, with even margins above and below tie. Tack in place. Tie together with knot at back, allowing ends to dangle down. Also tack knot in place.

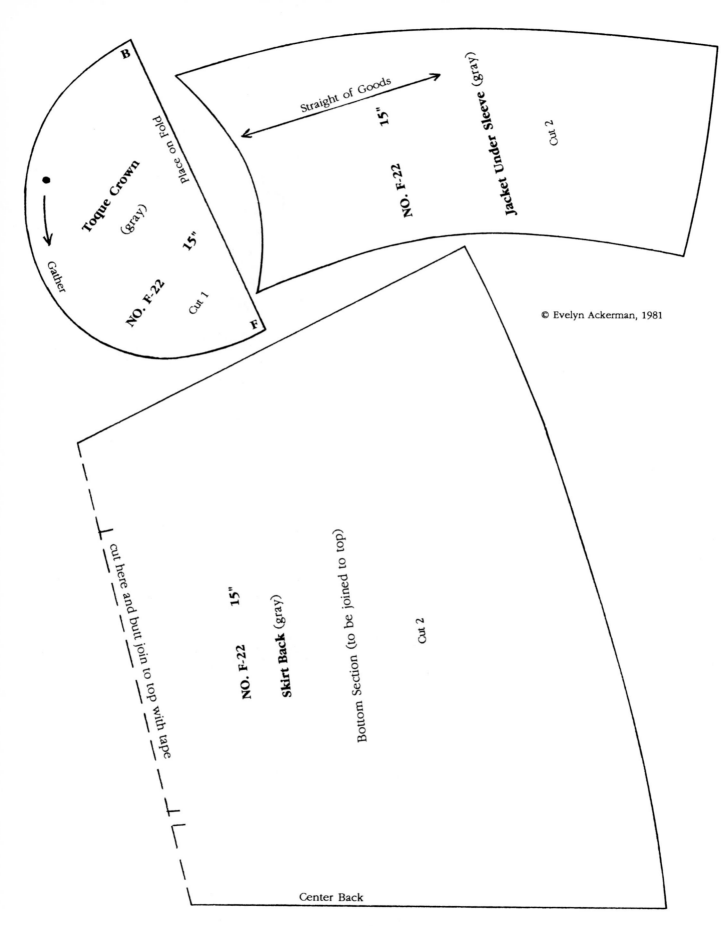

B

Toque Crown
(gray)

Place on Fold

15"

NO. F-22

Cut 1

F

Gather

Straight of Goods

15"

NO. F-22

Jacket Under Sleeve (gray)

Cut 2

© Evelyn Ackerman, 1981

cut here and butt join to top with tape

15"

NO. F-22

Skirt Back (gray)

Bottom Section (to be joined to top)

Cut 2

Center Back

78

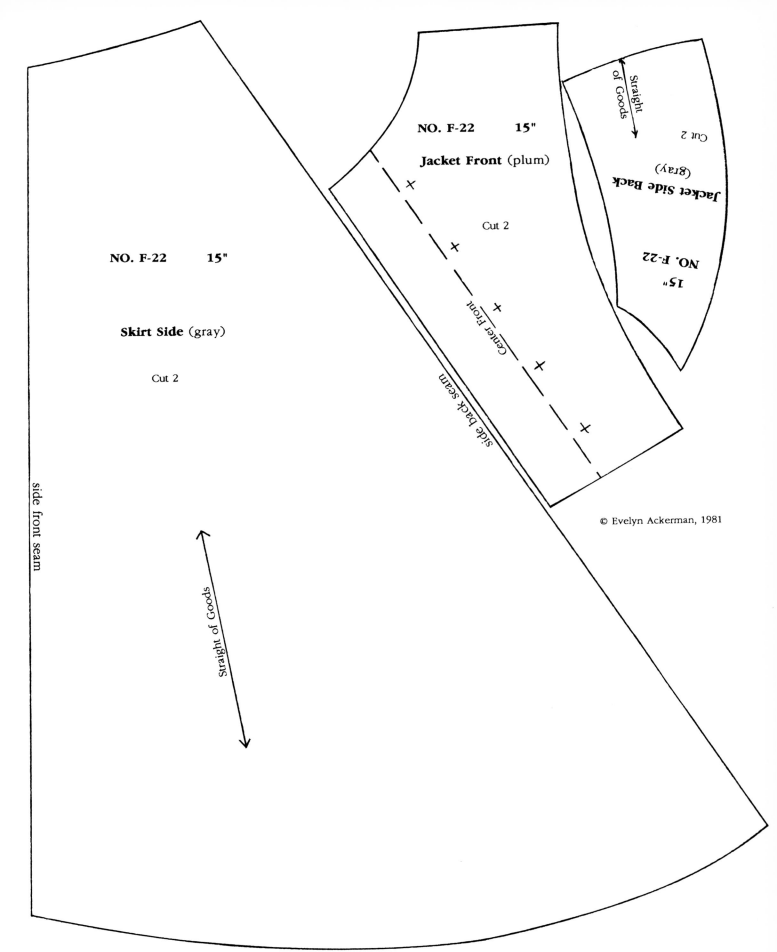

NO. F-22   **15"**

Jacket Front (plum)

Cut 2

Center Front

side back seam

NO. F-22   **15"**

Skirt Side (gray)

Cut 2

side front seam

Straight of Goods

Straight of Goods

Cut 2

Jacket Side Back (gray)

15"   **NO. F-22**

© Evelyn Ackerman, 1981

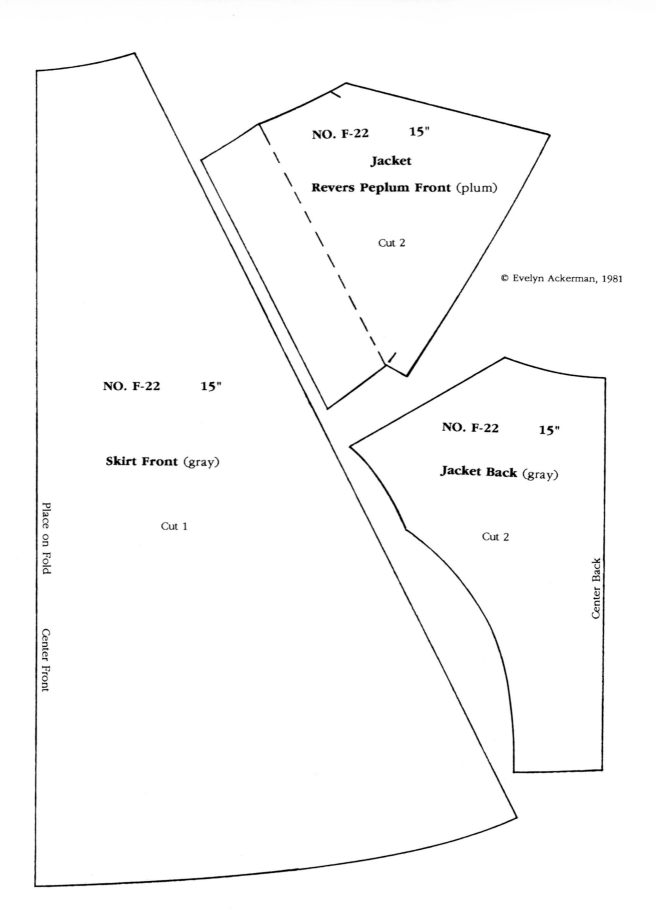

NO. F-22   15"

Jacket

Revers Peplum Front (plum)

Cut 2

© Evelyn Ackerman, 1981

NO. F-22   15"

Skirt Front (gray)

Cut 1

NO. F-22   15"

Jacket Back (gray)

Cut 2

Place on Fold   Center Front

Center Back

80

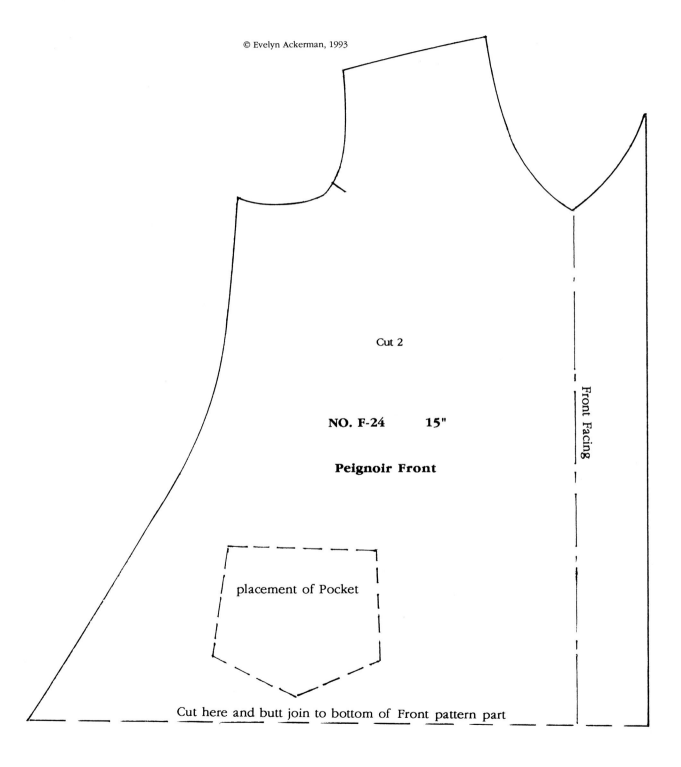

© Evelyn Ackerman, 1993

Cut 2

NO. F-24   15"

Peignoir Front

Front Facing

placement of Pocket

Cut here and butt join to bottom of Front pattern part

PATTERN NO. F-26
FOR A 13 INCH FASHION DOLL'S BLOUSE

General Instructions

• All pattern parts include 1/8" seams, with some made into French seams. Hems are also narrow.

• Press all seams and hems as work proceeds.

• Use fine, white cotton, such as cambric, batiste or lawn to make the blouse. Trim with narrow white lace, narrow white cotton eyelet or narrow white-on-white embroidered tape which has one scalloped edge.

Blouse

1. With wrong sides together, sew (close to raw edge) fronts to back at side seams. Press and turn to wrong side. Sew narrow seam, thus forming closed French seam.

2. Repeat step 1 for shoulder seams.

3. Place right side of shawl collar against wrong side of blouse, matching center back and top front corners.

Baste in place. Cut bias strip 5/8" wide and slightly longer than neckline. Place bias strip only against neckline of collar/blouse, turning back the end side hems and taking care not to catch these into seam along center fronts. Forming narrow seam, sew all parts in place, beginning at left bottom front and ending at right bottom front. Turn shawl collar to right side. Press. Turn under hem of bias strip and sew in place, concealing raw seam at neckline.

4. Turn under narrow hem along entire raw edge of shawl collar and press in place. Place narrow edge trim of your choice against edge of shawl collar and sew in place, using a butt-joint.

5. Sew tiny gathering stitches between dots of both sleeve cap and sleeve bottom. For wristband, cut rectangle of blouse fabric approximately 1-1/2" high and 1/2" wider than doll's hand (allowing for side seams and fit over hand). With right sides together, gather sleeve bottom and fit to wristband. Sew in place. Press. Bend wristband in half and hem in place on wrong side of sleeve. Place narrow edge trim (as per shawl collar edge) against bottom edge of wristband and sew in place with butt-joint. Repeat for other sleeve.

6. With right sides together sew sleeve underarm seam. With wrong side of blouse facing you and sleeve turned to right side, gather cap to fit armhole opening and match sleeve seam to front notch; pin sleeve in place. Adjust. Sew sleeve in place. Repeat for other sleeve.

7. Sew three buttons and three button loops at center-front opening, evenly spaced about 1" apart, beginning at top of blouse.

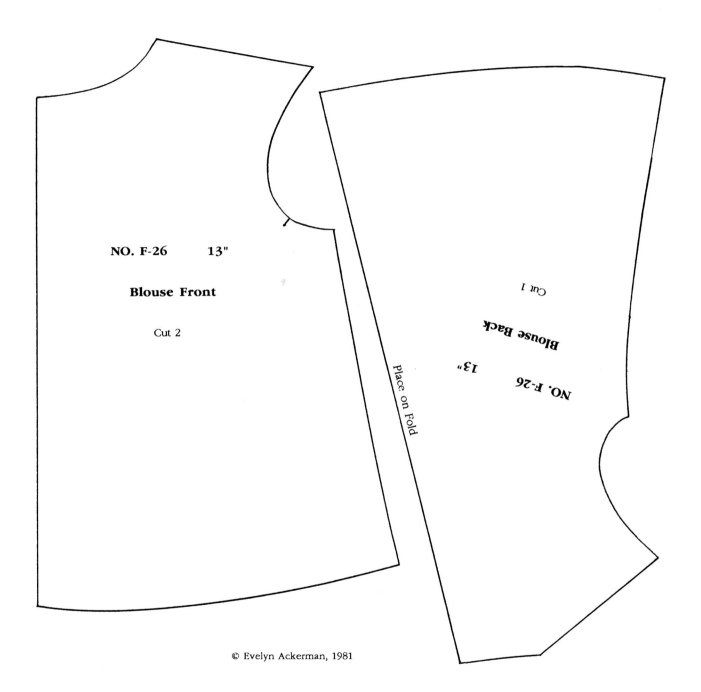

NO. F-26   13"

Blouse Front

Cut 2

Place on Fold

Cut 1

Blouse Back

13"

NO. F-26

© Evelyn Ackerman, 1981

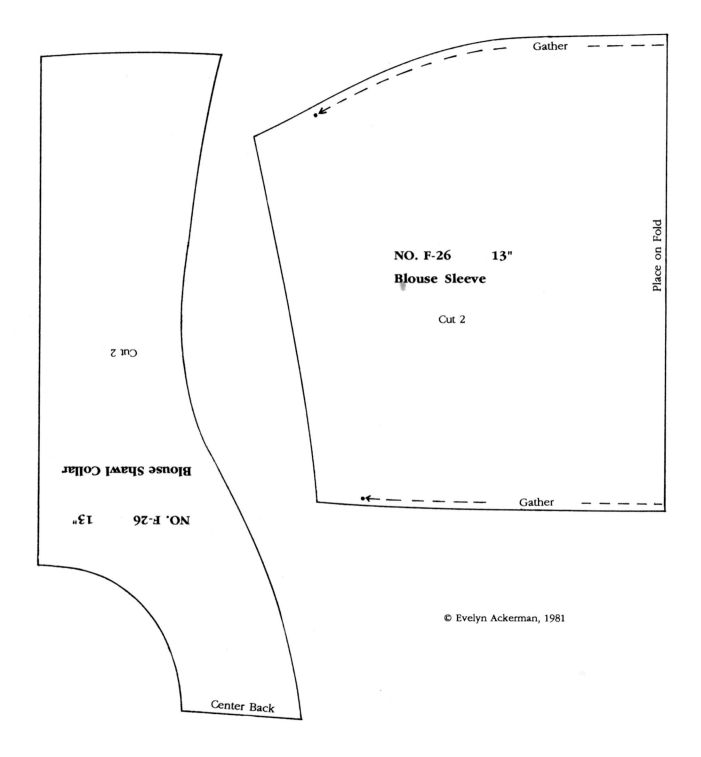

NO. F-26   13"

Blouse Sleeve

Cut 2

Place on Fold

Gather

Gather

Cut 2

Blouse Shawl Collar

NO. F-26   13"

Center Back

© Evelyn Ackerman, 1981

PATTERN NO. F-27 FOR A 13 INCH
FASHION DOLL'S FIGARO JACKET AND SKIRT

General Instructions

- All pattern parts include 3/16" seams and hems, unless otherwise noted.
- Press all seams and hems as work proceeds.
- The most suitable fabrics are either finely woven wools, silks, velvet or linen. Use solid colors. Trim is narrow, flat braid in color of fabric.

Figaro Jacket

1. With right sides together, sew center-back seam of backs.

2. With right sides together, sew sides to back, easing in fullness.

3. With right sides together, sew sides to fronts.

4. With right sides together, sew long seam of sleeve. About 1/2" above bottom, on right side, sew two rows of braid. With right sides together, sew other sleeve seam. Repeat for other sleeve.

5. With wrong side of jacket facing you and sleeve turned to right side, fit sleeve into armhole, matching short sleeve seam to jacket front notch. Ease in fullness while pinning in place for smooth fit. Sew sleeve in place. Repeat for other sleeve.

6. About 1/2" from jacket edge (not at neckline), on right side, sew two rows of braid.

7. Except for use of braid, repeat steps 1-5 for jacket lining.

8. With right sides together, matching seams, sew jacket lining to jacket, leaving most of neckline raw (for turning). Trim seams and corners. Turn to right side. Press. Turn under raw neckline hems and handstitch together. Press.

9. Turn under bottom hems of sleeves and sew in place.

10. Sew hook and eye at top center-front opening.

Skirt

1. From jacket fabric, cut rectangle 8" wide x 23" long.

2. With right sides together, from bottom, sew center-back seam half way. Press seam and center-back opening in place at one time. Sew center-back opening hem in place.

3. Along one long edge (waistline), form eight box pleats with each having a finished width of about 13/16". Pin in place.

4. With right sides together, sew waistband lining to waistband along sides and top edge (leave bottom open). Trim seams and corners. Turn and press.

5. With right sides together, fit pleated edge of skirt to waistband. Adjust pleats, if necessary. Sew in place, but avoid catching in waistband lining.

6. On wrong side, at waistline seam, turn under hem of waistband lining and handstitch in place.

7. Fit skirt to doll and turn under skirt's bottom hem. Handstitch in place.

8. On right side of skirt, attach two rows of braid near sewing line of hem. Also attach braid to waistband as an outline shape.

9. Sew hook and eye at center-back opening of waistband.

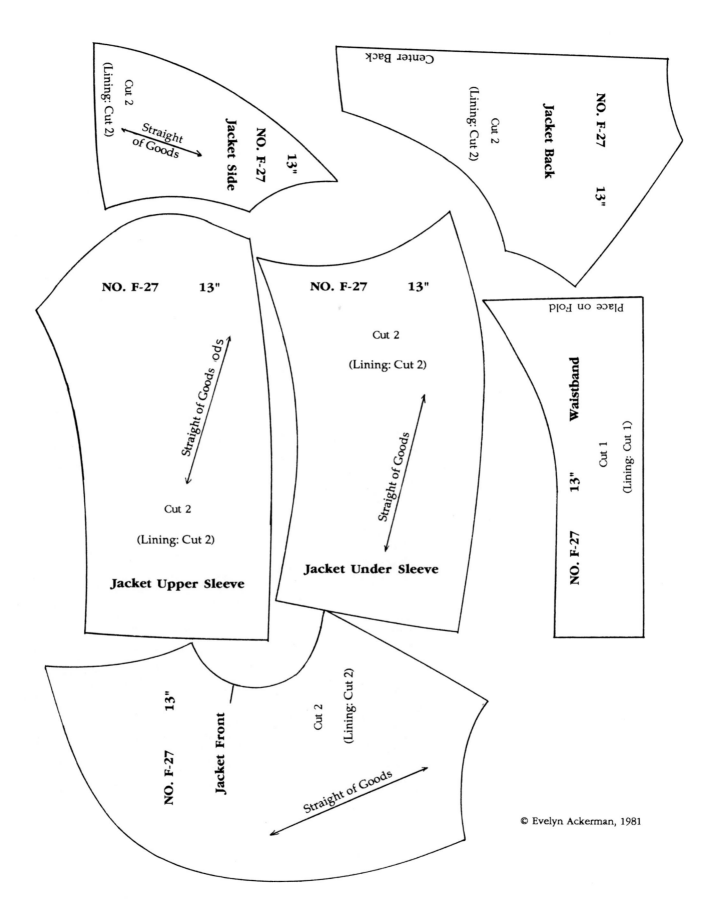

NO. F-27   13"

Jacket Side

Cut 2

(Lining: Cut 2)

Straight of Goods

Center Back

NO. F-27   13"

Jacket Back

Cut 2

(Lining: Cut 2)

Place on Fold

Waistband

Cut 1

(Lining: Cut 1)

NO. F-27   13"

NO. F-27   13"

Cut 2

(Lining: Cut 2)

Straight of Goods

Jacket Upper Sleeve

NO. F-27   13"

Cut 2

(Lining: Cut 2)

Straight of Goods

Jacket Under Sleeve

NO. F-27   13"

Jacket Front

Cut 2

(Lining: Cut 2)

Straight of Goods

© Evelyn Ackerman, 1981

94

PATTERN NO. F-28 FOR A 14 INCH
FASHION DOLL'S WINTER SUIT, BLOUSE AND HAT

General Instructions

- All pattern parts include 1/4" seams and hems, unless otherwise noted.
- Press all seams and hems as work proceeds.
- Chic and sophisticated in her elegant two-piece fall suit, with matching hat, the 1469 (a Simon & Halbig mold), Cuno & Otto Dressel doll is suitably dressed for lunch with the "girls," a teatime soirée or a career job. The combination of a flat-chested, boyish design with an ultra feminine effect is admirably achieved by the box-like construction of the suit, but effectively counterbalanced through the deceptively simple device of luxurious fur and rich fabrics.
- If wool is the preferred fabric (as per illustrated example), choices are available in a wide range of solid colors, as well as patterns—such as a houndstooth check, herringbone or plaid. Should a dressier type of suit be desired, the use of velvet would achieve this effect. Indeed, the possible variations, based on fabric used, appear to be endless. Regardless of which fabric is used, it should always be soft and pliable. When using patterned fabrics, a more professional appearance is achieved if all the parts of the pattern match at seams.
- The versatility of this pattern easily permits it to be used to enlarge the doll's wardrobe. By lengthening the suit jacket, for example, the seamstress can create a coat. Further changes in appearance can be achieved by applying fur only at the collar (which would require making the jacket facing from the jacket fabric), eliminating the fur and opening the sleeve bottom with a slit and adding a button. Simple alterations effectively can be the basis for an entirely different ensemble.
- The suit's belt buckle is recycled from an old doll's shoe-bow, but if no

such object is available, one can be cut from a piece of leather.

• The 1920s design thrust is further implemented by the soft folds, shirred details, and other design features of what is essentially a straight-cut, sea-green silk blouse—a subtle color which maintains the subdued tones of the plaid suit. The versatility of this design permits the pattern (like that of the jacket) to be used to enlarge the doll's wardrobe. Nothing more complicated need be done to the blouse than lengthen it to make a dress. Further changes can be created by changing the trim (such as adding ties to the bodice), shortening the sleeves, contrasting the fabric color of the top overlay with that of the bodice and sleeves.

Wrap-around Skirt

1. As per pattern, on wrong side of skirt rectangle, baste in place the three back darts. Sew and press.
2. Turn in both side facings. Sew in place and press.
3. Cut a waistband from skirt fabric, 3/4" wide and slightly longer than top raw edge of skirt (after facings and darts are sewn in place). With right sides together, sew waistband to skirt top; trim seam; press. Turn waistband in half lengthwise, allowing for hemming on wrong side, to inside of skirt. Then turn in both sides; handstitch closed. Hem waistband to inside of skirt.
4. Fit skirt to the doll (the darts should be centered at the back of the doll) and sew two snaps at waistband. While the skirt is on doll, turn under bottom hem to desired length. Baste in place. Handstitch; press.

Jacket

1. With right sides together, using a 1/8" seam, sew a pocket lining to one pocket at the top and the side that will be facing the jacket's center front. Trim seams and corners; turn to right sides. Matching raw edges of pocket bottom and side (pocket lining on inside) to raw edges of jacket front bottom and

side, pin pocket in place. Topstitch pocket to jacket along the pocket's seamed side. Repeat for other pocket, which will face in the opposite direction.
2. With right sides together, sew jacket fronts to jacket back at side seams; press. Repeat for jacket lining.
3. With right sides together, sew jacket shoulder seams; press. Repeat for jacket lining.
4. With right sides together, sew both sleeve underarm seams; press. Repeat for sleeve linings.
5. With wrong side of jacket facing you and sleeve turned to the right side, fit sleeve into armhole. Match sleeve underarm seam to jacket side seam. Easing in any fullness, pin sleeve in place while adjusting for smooth fit. Handstitch in place. Repeat for other sleeve; then repeat for jacket sleeve linings.
6. Fit jacket to doll and turn under sleeve hems to desired length. On wrong side, baste sleeve hems in place.
7. With right sides together, using a 1/8" seam, sew collar lining to collar on the rounded edge only. Turn and press. With right sides together, matching raw necklines and using a 1/8" seam, sew collar to jacket; press.
8. Fit jacket (and sleeves) to jacket lining (and sleeve linings), wrong sides together. Match underarm and shoulder seams; pin together at these points. Turn in front facings and bottom hem of jacket; baste in place.
9. Turn under all hems of jacket lining to fit jacket (including neckline) and pin in place. Handstitch in place. Press.
10. Cut—using a sharp, single-edged razor blade—a strip of fur on skin side, approximately 3/4" to 1" wide, and long enough to fit the jacket from left bottom edge, around collar, to right bottom edge. Fit to the lining side of jacket, fur facing right side out, matching one long edge of skin to outer edge of jacket lining. Overcast the edges together. Using a running stitch, attach other long side of skin's edge to lining. Fold so that fur faces right side out of jacket.

11. Cut a piece of jacket fabric 3/4" wide x 11-1/2" long to make a belt. (Finished size will be approximately 3/8" wide x 11" long.) Finish the belt by cross-stitching the long sides together at the center of the belt underside. Turn in ends and sew closed. Press. Fit belt to jacket while on doll and place buckle so it is at center front. Use a snap to hold the belt closed.
12. At jacket side seams, sew thread-constructed buttonhole loop from dot and above pocket, making sure the loop is wide enough to hold belt. (The belt, when in place and buckled, should fall just across pocket tops.)

Hat

1. For hat crown, cut a circle of suit fabric 6-1/2" in diameter. For hat band, cut a rectangle of the same fabric 1-3/4" wide x 6" long.
2. Fit band to head and baste center-back seam. Trim seam of any excess. Sew one or two rows of gathering stitches around entire circumference of crown. Gather to fit band. With right sides together, baste crown to band. Place hat on doll to ensure a proper fit. Sew center-back seam and crown in place; press.
3. Place hat on doll's head. Pin puff of crown down around the band on the left and right sides of doll's forehead. When satisfied with the appearance, tack in place. Add rosette, bow or other decorative device where wanted.

Blouse

1. With right sides of front overlay against wrong side of blouse front, matching raw shoulder seams and front "V," sew "V" neck seam. Clip at point and turn to right side; press.
2. Turn under 1/8" hems along raw edges (clip as per pattern); first press and baste, then topstitch in place.
3. With right sides together, matching raw necklines, sew back facings to backs. Turn to wrong sides; press.
4. Handstitch rows of vertical gathering stitches on front (three rows—at center and about 3/4" from each side; see pattern).

5. With right sides together, sew shoulder seams; press.

6. With right sides together, baste side seams from bottom to bottom of gathering stitches. Baste side seams from armhole opening to top of gathering stitches. Pull gathering stitches into position (medium tension) and also fold horizontal front pleat into place (adjust gathering stitches until all fit in place with side seams of front matching those of backs. First baste, then sew in place; press.

7. Press in place 1/8" top hem of lower sleeve overlay. Baste to sleeve, matching top of basted hem to correct position (as per pattern of dotted line on sleeve). Topstitch in place. Repeat for other sleeve.

8. With right sides together, sew sleeve underarm seam. With wrong side of blouse armhole facing you and sleeve turned to right side, match underarm seam of sleeve to side seam of blouse. Pin sleeve into armhole, easing in any fullness for smooth fit. Handstitch in place. Repeat for other sleeve. Fit blouse to doll and turn under both sleeve hems to desired sleeve length. On wrong side, handstitch sleeve hems in place.

9. From bottom to dot sew center-back seam. Turn under hems of center-back opening and handstitch in place.

10. Sew buttonhole loop and button near neckline of center-back opening.

11. Fit blouse to doll and turn under bottom hem. Handstitch in place and press.

View of blouse.

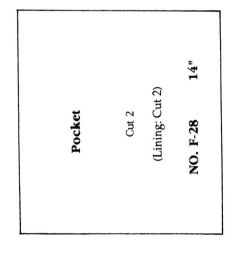

Pocket

Cut 2

(Lining: Cut 2)

NO. F-28   14"

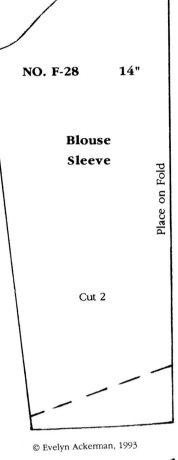

NO. F-28   14"

Blouse Sleeve

Cut 2

Place on Fold

© Evelyn Ackerman, 1993

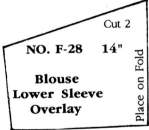

Cut 2

NO. F-28   14"

Blouse Lower Sleeve Overlay

Place on Fold

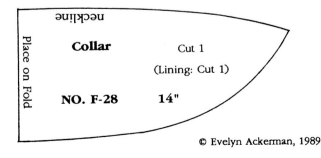

neckline

Collar   Cut 1

(Lining: Cut 1)

NO. F-28   14"

Place on Fold

© Evelyn Ackerman, 1989

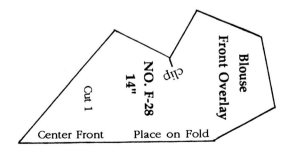

Blouse Front Overlay

clip

NO. F-28 14"

Cut 1

Center Front   Place on Fold

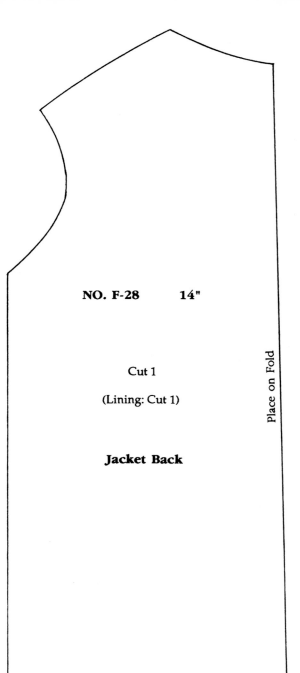

NO. F-28   14"

Cut 1

(Lining: Cut 1)

Jacket Back

Place on Fold

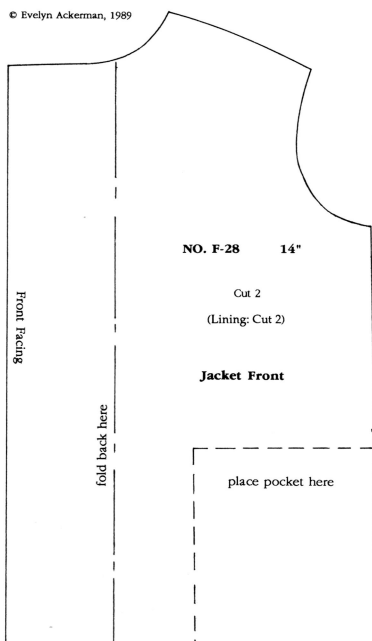

Front Facing

NO. F-28   14"

Cut 2

(Lining: Cut 2)

Jacket Front

fold back here

place pocket here

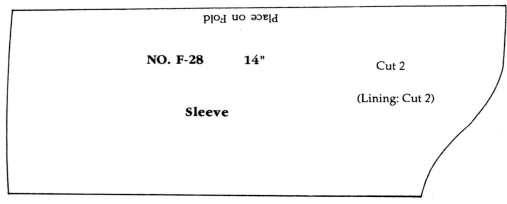

Place on Fold

NO. F-28   14"

Cut 2

(Lining: Cut 2)

Sleeve

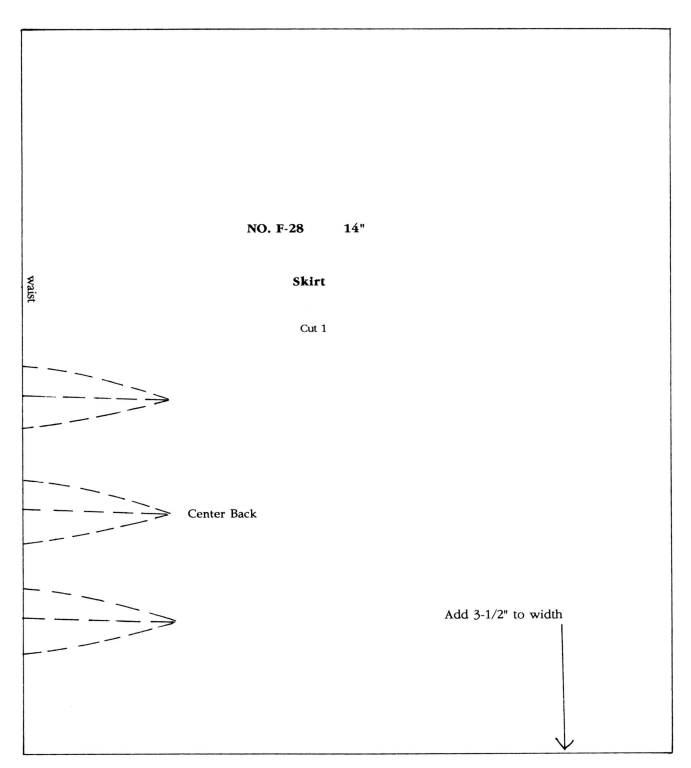

NO. F-28   14"

Skirt

Cut 1

waist

Center Back

Add 3-1/2" to width

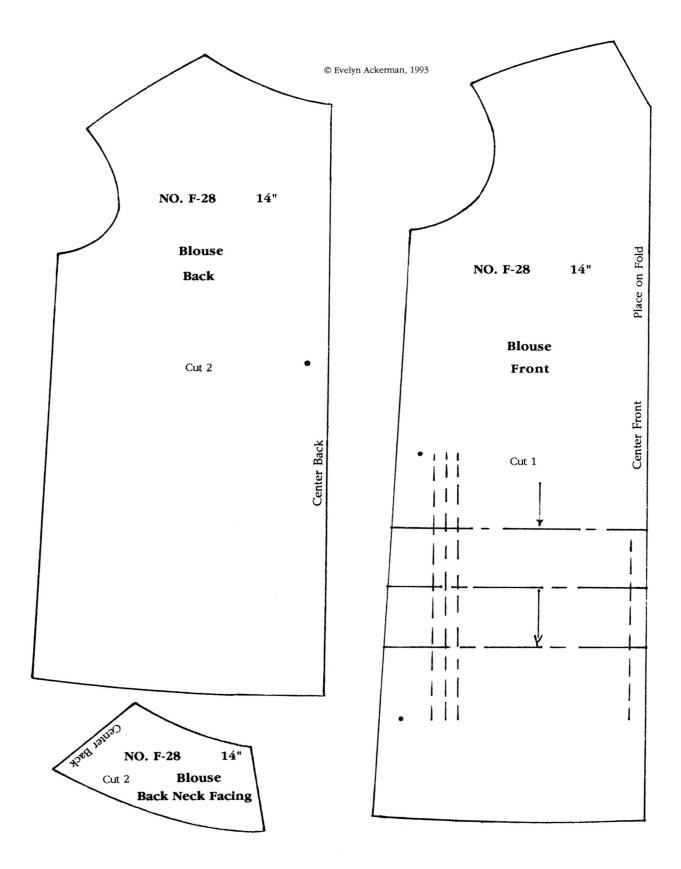

© Evelyn Ackerman, 1993

NO. F-28   14"

Blouse

Back

Cut 2

Center Back

NO. F-28   14"

Blouse
Front

Place on Fold

Center Front

Cut 1

Center Back

NO. F-28   14"

Cut 2   Blouse
Back Neck Facing

100

PATTERN NO. F-29
FOR A 14 INCH FASHION DOLL'S LOUNGEWEAR

General Instructions

• All pattern parts include 1/4" seams and hems, unless otherwise noted.

• Press all seams and hems as work proceeds.

• Many fabrics available in the 1920s are suitable, such as rayon, cotton, silk jersey and satin. As the illustrated garment shows, a printed fabric can be very appealing. A combination of a print and solid color, contrasting solid colors or the use of a single color can also be effective. Whatever the choice, the fabric used should be flexible and have the ability to drape naturally for the best fit.

Pants

1. With right sides together, sew center-front seam from dot to waistline.

2. With right sides together, sew center-back seam from dot to waistline.

3. With right sides together, match center-front seam to center-back seam. Sew inside pant legs from bottom of one side, around curve, to bottom of other side. Reinforce seam at crotch. Clip curves.

Bodice

1. With right sides together, sew bodice fronts to bodice back at side seams.

2. With right sides together, sew shoulder seams.

3. With right sides together, pin bodice waistline to pant waistline at sides, matching underarm side seams to fold representing pant side seams. Turn under center-front facings of bodice so that center-fronts meet in butt joint, or fit garment to doll and just slightly overlap the two bodice front parts at waistline and pin in place, adjusting center-front facings so bodice/pants are not a skin-tight fit. Remove from doll. Sew all parts in place.

4. Either the pattern for the short collar (illustrated) or the long collar can be used. With right sides together, using 1/8" seams, sew collar to collar lining, except at raw neckline. Trim seam and corners. Clip curves. Turn collar to right side. Press so that the seam line does not show on collar side.

5. Cut bias strip (from garment fabric) 5/8" wide by length that is at least 3/8" longer than raw neckline. With right sides out, place collar neckline at bodice neckline, matching center-backs. Baste in place. With right sides together, sew 1/8" seam through bias strip, collar and bodice (at neckline). Turn bias strip to wrong side, press and trim the length of its raw edge so that when finished, it is hemmed but narrow. Handstitch in place, with raw ends turned under.

6. Note that there is a choice for sleeve style. With right sides together, sew sleeve seam. Repeat for other sleeve. If sleeve is left with bell shape, as per illustrated garment (opening at wrist wide like opening of pant bottom), turn under bottom hem and handstitch in place. Repeat for other sleeve. If sleeve is gathered at bottom to fit sleeve band, sew side seams of sleeve band with right sides together. Sleeve band opening must fit over hand. With right sides together, matching side seams, fit gathering of sleeve bottom to sleeve band. Sew in place. Repeat for other sleeve.

7. With sleeve turned to right side and bodice turned to wrong side, fit sleeve into armhole opening, matching underarm seam of sleeve to side seam of bodice. Pin in place, easing in fullness for smooth fit. Sew in place. Repeat for other sleeve.

8. Place garment on doll and pin bottom of pants to desired length. Adjust and remove from doll. Baste in place along line of pant bottom. Turn under bottom hem and handstitch in place.

9. Cut rectangle for belt 1-1/2" wide x 9-1/2" long. With right sides together, bend belt in half. Sew 1/8" seam length of belt. Turn to right side

and adjust so seam is at center of belt. Press. Turn under raw ends and hand-stitch in place. Fit buckle of appropriate color and size to left side of belt and sew in place after bending end over belt bar. Across waistline seam, by side seams, sew belt loops wide enough to receive belt. These can be made of cloth or thread, although the latter is easier to handle.

10. At center front of bodice, sew 4 evenly spaced buttonhole loops on right side and 4 buttons to match on left side.

11. For hair band, cut fabric rectangle 2" wide x 14" long. With right sides together, bend in half and sew 1/8" wide long seam. Turn to right side and press with seam at center on wrong side of hair band. Turn under raw ends and handstitch in place. When tied in place around head, the excess band will be just long enough to be tied with knot so that band extensions form simulated bow-tie.

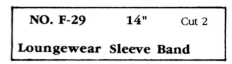

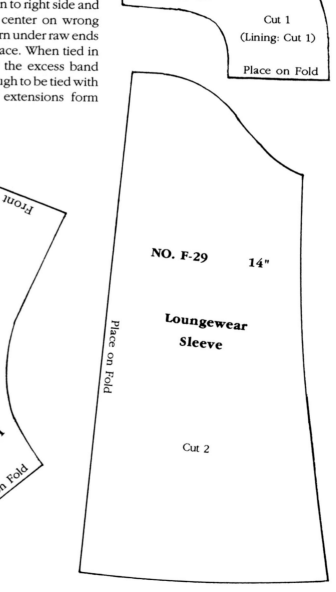

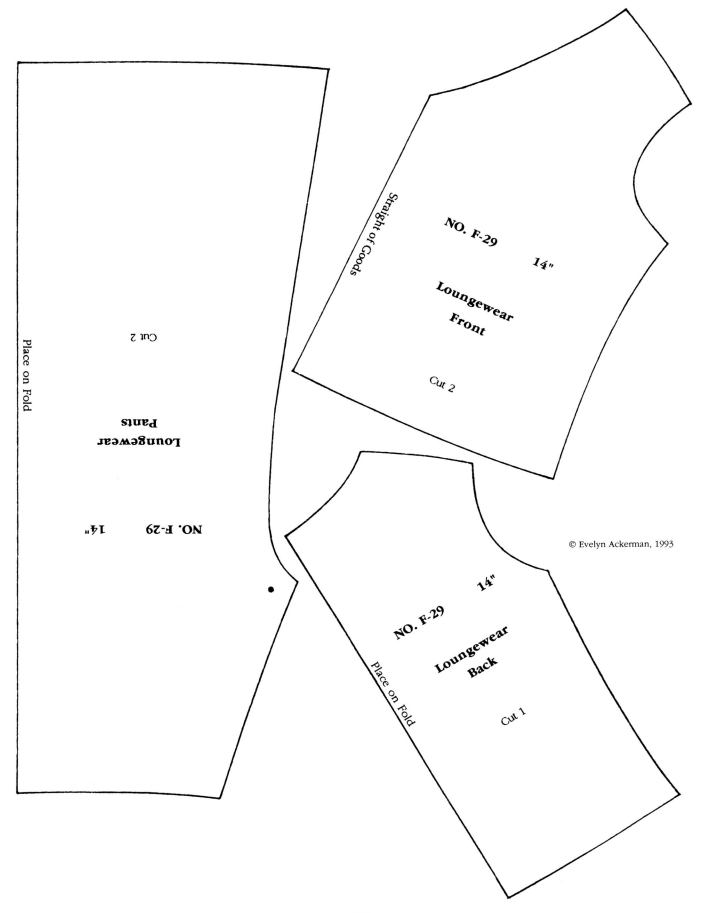

Place on Fold

Cut 2

Loungewear Pants

NO. F-29   14"

Straight of Goods

NO. F-29   14"

Loungewear
Front

Cut 2

© Evelyn Ackerman, 1993

14"

NO. F-29

Loungewear
Back

Place on Fold

Cut 1

PART IV

Hats for Antique Dolls

PATTERN NO. H-35
FOR A 9-1/2 TO 11 INCH GIRL DOLL'S HAT

Considerable interest can be added to the appearance of a doll by means of a well-chosen hat. The possibilities are endless, with variations limited only by one's imagination. Some of the illustrated patterns are simple to make, while others call for more skill and ingenuity, but all are possible for the patient and determined. Since these patterns are based on research of original hats worn by antique dolls between 1870 and 1915, the reward for effort involved will be a well loved doll whose beauty is enhanced by a hat that accurately simulates an antique style.

The choice of fabric is crucial to the final results. Obviously, it would be ideal if cloth of the same age as the doll could be used, but since this is rarely possible, it is essential that the modern fabric chosen recalls the earlier one both in appearance and fiber content. Synthetics cannot accomplish this and should not be used. Therefore, use fabrics made of natural fibers,

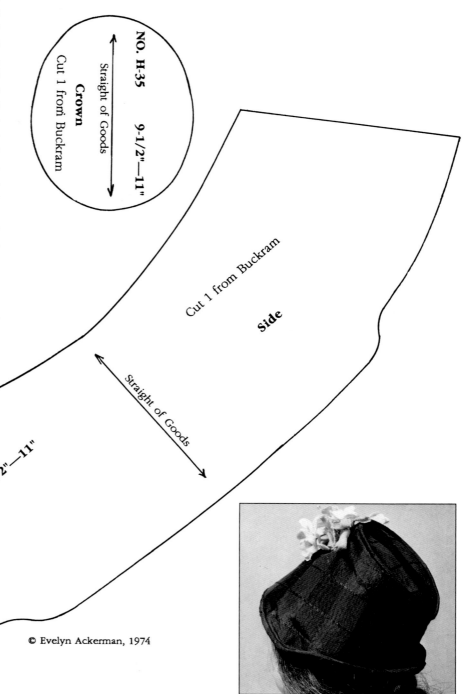

NO. H-35   9-1/2"—11"

Crown
Cut 1 from Buckram

Straight of Goods

Cut 1 from Buckram

Side

Straight of Goods

NO. H-35   9-1/2"—11"

© Evelyn Ackerman, 1974

Back view.

106

such as silk, cotton, velvet, faille, taffeta, wool or plush. Trims, too, are most important for a hat and a correct choice, in the right scale to the doll and hat fabric, with colors of all component parts well related—even subtle— will create an accessory in the doll's wardrobe that not only will evoke an authentic appearance, but will make her truly well dressed.

The basic supplies used in the making of many of these hats, such as milliner's wire (a wrapped, flexible wire that is available in different gauges), buckram or similar textiles, are not always readily available, except in large metropolitan areas. These materials can be found in milliner supply houses, large suppliers of fab-rics and notions for the seamstress and some department stores. It is also necessary to have on hand a wire cutter's tool, available from many hardware stores or suppliers of jewelers' tools.

Buckram Pattern Parts

1. Cut pattern parts as shown in buckram.
2. Overlap center-back seam of hat side (fit to doll and adjust) and sew in place.
3. Butt-join hat side at top (narrower than bottom) to hat crown and overcast stitch side to crown at butt joint.
4. Attach milliner's wire to bottom edge of hat side (on top side), using an overcast stitch and overlapping wire about 1/4" at bottom back, securing overlap firmly in place.

Fabric Pattern Parts

1. Cut bias strip from fabric, approximately 1/2" wide and slightly longer than bottom of hat. With right side facing out, bend bias strip over wire front and back (around circumference of hat bottom). Using tiny running stitches, handstitch as close to wire as possible, thus creating the effect of a piped edge. Do not trim off excess fabric raw edge (facing up on inside and outside of hat side).
2. For lining of hat side, cut a bias rectangle slightly larger than pattern part. Turning under one long hem, attach first at hat bottom along running stitch at wire ("piped" edge). Then tack upper section in place.
3. For lining of hat crown, cut fabric larger than pattern part, allowing for turned under hems around its edge. Place fabric lining on inside of crown and sew turned under hems in place to hat side lining.
4. For crown, cut hat fabric larger than pattern part. Place fabric on crown, right side out, pin in place with extra fabric extending over hat side. Attach in place with running stitch along top edge of hat side.
5. To make piping for crown edge, cut hat fabric bias strip 1/2" wide and slightly longer than crown circumference. Place narrow cord on wrong side in center of bias strip. Bend strip in half, with right sides out. Handstitch tiny running stitches as close to cord as possible, enclosing cord. Handstitch cord as close to top edge, where crown and side meet, with raw edge of piping facing down on hat side.
6. For hat side, cut bias rectangle slightly bigger than pattern part, allowing for top and bottom hems. Fit smoothly in place, pinning first to allow for necessary placement adjustments. Slipstitch top, bottom and center-back seam in place.
7. Attach ornamental trim, such as flowers, ribbon, feathers, as shown or as desired. Turn up bottom-back portion of hat side.

PATTERN NO. H-36
FOR A 12 TO 13 INCH GIRL DOLL'S HAT

General Instructions

• This hat looks best made in an easily draped fabric that has some weight, such as velvet or velour. Other fabrics are needed for hat bottom and lining (read instructions). Trim choice is optional, but a floral sprig is appropriate.

• Buckram and milliner's wire are required.

Hat

1. At center back, overlap buckram, forming seam. Handstitch in place.

2. Attach milliner's wire to bottom edge of buckram (on top side), using an overcast stitch and overlapping wire about 1/4" at bottom back. Secure wire ends in place.

3. Bend a double thickness of thin hat fabric (use a color and texture that is complementary to main hat fabric) over buckram, from bottom up 1", both inside and outside. Smooth into place and tack front through back along top raw edge. Form an overlapping seam at center back and sew in place.

4. For lining of hat, cut rectangle of fabric (such as china silk), 1-1/2" wide x 8-1/2" long. Turn under hem along long edge and handstitch to top of inside fabric. Overlap center-back seam and tack seam in place. Turn under hem along remaining long raw edge and sew tiny running stitch the entire length. Pull, gathering this into a small circle and knotting ends firmly in place.

This constitutes lining for hat crown.

5. Turn under bottom hem of hat side fabric (e.g., velvet) and handstitch in place (do not attach to hat). Pin to cover buckram, leaving about 1/2" to 5/8" of fabric covering buckram along bottom part exposed. Be sure to match center fronts and center backs.

6. Turn under 1/8" hem along top edge of hat side fabric. Matching center fronts and center backs, pin crown to side top, slipping raw edge of crown under top hem of side. Adjust puckers to suit taste. Crown will pouf up a bit. Handstitch in place.

7. Add ornamental trim, such as flowers and leaves, to hat.

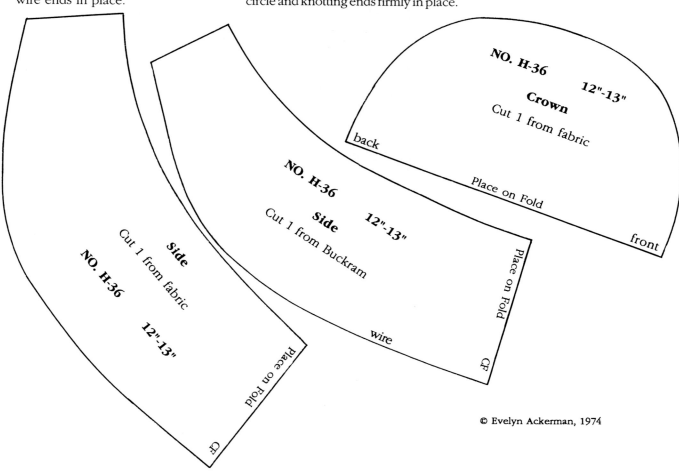

NO. H-36 12"-13" Crown Cut 1 from fabric — back — Place on Fold — front — Place on Fold — CF

NO. H-36 Side Cut 1 from Buckram 12"-13" — wire

Side Cut 1 from fabric NO. H-36 12"-13" — Place on Fold — CF

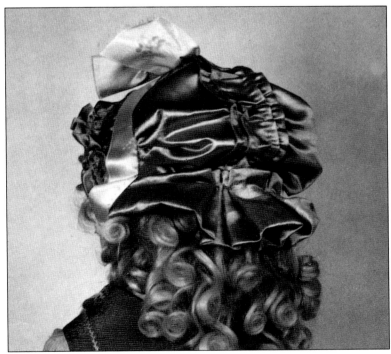

PATTERN NO. H-43
FOR A 16 TO 18 INCH FASHION DOLL'S HAT

General Instructions

• Suitable fabrics include a wide range of ones made from natural fibers, such as wool, velvet, satin, taffeta, faille, velour and brocade. Band can be made from same fabric as hat. Silk or satin ribbon can be substituted for this. As shown, the hat also includes transparent glass beads and a steel button, but other trims can be added or substituted, such as feathers.

• Lining fabric is required (glazed cotton, linen or silk are the fabrics of choice).

• A medium weight milliner's wire and buckram are also required.

Hat

1. Cut crown pattern part from buckram. On outer edge, cut slits inward as per lines on pattern part. Form pie-shaped wedges by crossing buckram edges of each slit, with widest wedges at front of crown. Gradually taper the width of wedges as they reach the back. Pin in place. Adjust for softly shaped crown that has the most vertical downward turn at front and a gently sloping one at back. When desired shape is achieved, handstitch these pie-shaped wedges firmly in place.

2. Cut brim pattern part from buckram. Along inner edge, cut slits approximately 1/4" deep and spaced approximately 1/4" apart around entire inner circumference of brim. Using fingers, bend slit edge up and form a 1/4" deep lip. Fit brim to bottom of crown, matching center fronts and bottom edge of crown with bent edge of brim. Pin in place and overlap center-back seam of brim (trim excess, if necessary, but allow for sufficient overlap). Sew brim to crown at bent-up lip and secure center-back seam of brim in place.

3. Using wire cutters, cut milliner's wire 3/4" longer than entire outer edge of brim. Beginning at center back, place milliner's wire on top of and next to outer edge of brim. As work proceeds, hold wire in place with fingers and sew it securely in place, using either an overcast or blanket stitch.

4. Cut one bias strip from hat fabric that is 1/2" wider than double the width of the brim and 1/2" longer than brim. With right side out, fold in half. Matching center front of bias strip and hat brim, place brim buckram between the half-fold of the bias strip (permitting half the bias strip to cover the top of the brim with an additional 1/4" excess to act as a lip that extends atop the lip of the brim's buckram). Like the lip of the buckram, the bias trim's lip must also be slit approximately 1/4" deep, but need not be cut as close together. Slitting the lip in this manner will allow for as smooth a fit of the fabric over the brim as possible. The excess bias on the bottom half will be used to cover the underside of the brim. Pin top half of brim fabric in place as fitting and adjusting of fabric to brim proceeds. When fabric is fitted as smoothly as possible, use small running stitches to sew fabric to buckram at bend of lip (where crown and brim meet). Also sew lip across its top (on crown). Pin bias strip in place on underside, adjusting it to fit brim. Using tiny running stitches that do not sew through bias fabric on front, sew underside bias half of brim fabric to bottom edge of crown.

5. From hat fabric, cut crown covering so that it is slightly wider than crown pattern part. Match straight of goods to straight center of pattern part. Place fabric over crown, right side out and matching fronts. Using fingers and matching fronts. Using fingers and pins, adjust to fit so all parts of crown are evenly covered and bottom edge of fabric matches bend of brim lip. Trim bottom edge if necessary. Using tiny running stitch, sew in place to buckram as close to bottom edge of crown fabric as possible.

6. From hat fabric (ribbon may be substituted), cut a rectangle of fabric at least 3/8" longer (or more) than circumference of crown bottom and wide enough so that finished width of band is 1/4" wide and turn-under hems are hidden. Using a beading needle, sew transparent beads about 1/4" apart along length of band, except for ends that will need to be butt-joined, knotted or tied. Pin band to hat so that connecting ends are at side of hat and raw seam of brim and crown are covered. Handstitch band to hat along both long edges. Sew steel button (or other decorative piece) to band at connection of band ends.

7. Optional: Fit hat to doll and pin chin ribbons in place (approximate center at sides of hat). Remove hat and securely sew the chin ribbons to hat. (Hat pins also can be used to hold hat to doll's head.)

8. For hat lining, cut a rectangle of fabric 2" wide x 8" long. Along both long edges turn under 1/8" and press in place. With right side out, place one long edge at stitching line of underside fabric of brim, matching center fronts. Pin in place. Allowing for center back seam of lining, handstitch lining to underside fabric of brim. Handstitch center-back seam of lining. As close as possible to other long edge of lining, sew tiny running stitches and pull to gather into a small circular opening. Using fingers, push lining into underside of hat crown, thus hiding all construction parts.

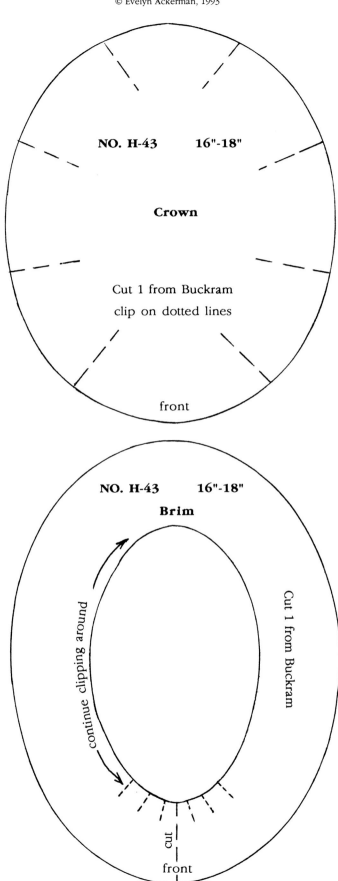

NO. H-43   16"-18"

Crown

Cut 1 from Buckram

clip on dotted lines

front

NO. H-43   16"-18"

Brim

continue clipping around

Cut 1 from Buckram

cut

front

115

PART V

Miniature Dolls

PATTERN NO. M-44
FOR A 6-1/4 INCH GIRL DOLL'S DRESS

General Instructions

- All pattern parts include 1/8" seams and hems, unless otherwise noted.
- Press all seams and hems as work proceeds.
- The fabric must be a type that existed at the end of the 19th century. Suitable fabrics are lightweight silk, silk taffeta, silk brocade, cotton or wool.
- Fabrics in pale colors were the ones generally used for main pattern parts. If a dress, such as the illustrated one, had a front insert, the insert could be made from a fabric with a deeper hued color that contrasted with the dress fabric or one with a pattern (such as a floral) in order to add a more decorative accent to the overall effect.
- A pale blue silk with a brocaded pattern is used for the illustrated dress. The insert, made from a matching, pale blue satin, provides a subtle contrast. Nineteenth century lace, approximately 5/16" wide, and beige satin ribbon, approximately 3/8" wide, are the only trims used. All pattern parts are lined with a gauze-like cotton. Although the illustrated garment is entirely handsewn, the use of sewing machine stitches is acceptable.

Dress

1. With right sides together, sew matching lining parts to each front and each back across bottom edge only. Turn to right side.
2. With right sides together, matching underarm openings and bottom edges, loosely baste fronts to backs at side seams to prevent non-alignment of parts. Sew in place.
3. With right sides together, matching necklines, sew back at center-back seam from neckline to large dot. Clip seam from top of pleat edge to large dot.
4. With right sides together, matching tops and bottoms, sew center-back pleat seam. Press pleat in place and tack across top to lining only.
5. With right sides together, sew shoulder seams.
6. Turn under front-opening hems about 1/16" from bottom to small dot. Sew in place.
7. With right sides together, sew insert lining to insert along right side from top to bottom, across bottom, then along left side from bottom to top. Turn to right side.
8. Fit insert to fronts so that bottom hems match. Turn in top hems, matching insert to + on front.
9. With right side out, place flat of straight edge of lace on top of and about 1/8" from front edge of dress: sew lace to dress by starting at left front bottom and continuing up and around neckline, then down right front to bottom.
10. Matching bottoms, tack insert (right side out) to right front (center opening) of dress at bottom (with right side of front overlapping insert about 1/8").
11. With right side out, place flat of straight edge of lace on top of and about 1/16" from bottom edge of dress and sew in place from open edge of insert across entire dress bottom.
12. Lightly gather a length of ribbon (that is slightly more than double the length of the dress bottom) by using two rows of tiny running stitches close together, along its top edge. Overlapping top of lace at bottom hemline, sew ribbon across dress bottom.
13. Sew strip of lace across insert top, with scalloped edge of lace above it by approximately 1/16".
14. Sew two strips of flat ribbon across insert, as per dotted pattern line, sewing only along top edge of ribbon.
15. Place lace (right side out) along inside raw edge of neckline from right side + to left side +, matching scalloped edges of outer and inner lace, thus covering raw edge of dress fabric.
16. Beginning at underarm seam, with right side of lace against right side of dress, matching straight edge of lace to raw edge of armhole, sew lace to armhole close to straight edge; end by sewing underarm seam of lace. Then along armhole edge, overcast stitch the armhole opening of dress and lace together for firmer attachment.
17. Fit dress to doll and pin insert in place at center front. When positioned properly, on wrong side, using a tiny running stitch, sew insert to right front. Sew insert to left front from bottom up no more than 1".
18. Sew two small hooks to underside of left front and handstitch eyes to matching place on insert for dress closure.

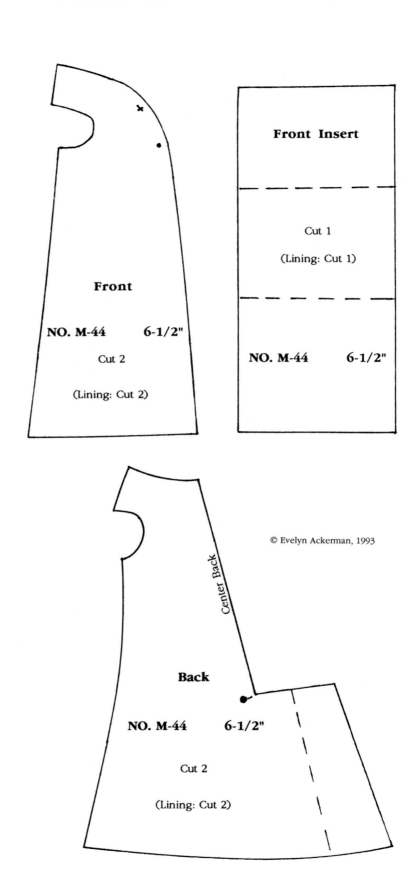

Front

NO. M-44   **6-1/2"**

Cut 2

(Lining: Cut 2)

Front Insert

Cut 1

(Lining: Cut 1)

NO. M-44   **6-1/2"**

Center Back

Back

NO. M-44   **6-1/2"**

Cut 2

(Lining: Cut 2)

© Evelyn Ackerman, 1993

120

PATTERN NO. M-47
FOR A 6 INCH GIRL DOLL'S DRESS

General Instructions

• All pattern parts include 1/8" seams and hems, unless otherwise noted.

• Press all seams and hems as work proceeds.

• Any lightweight, natural-fibered fabric is suitable, especially silk. Narrow lace and a length of slightly stiffened gauze are also required.

Dress

1. Cut off excess of left center-back opening as shown on pattern (left side at top is not gathered).

2. Turn under 1/4" bottom hem and handstitch in place.

3. Turn under both 1/4" center-back opening hems and handstitch in place.

4. With right sides together, sew shoulder seams.

5. Turn under neckline hem and press in place.

6. At each sleeve cap, sew gathering stitches. Turn under bottom of each sleeve hem and sew in place.

7. With right sides together, sew sleeve underarm seam. With wrong side of bodice facing you and the sleeve turned to the right side, put the sleeve into the armhole, matching top-center notch to shoulder seam and sleeve underarm seam to bodice side seam. Pin in place, easing in gathered cap to fit opening. Handstitch in place. Trim seam. Repeat for other sleeve.

8. Attach lace to inside of sleeve's bottom opening so that approximately 1/8" lace extends beyond sleeve bottom. Handstitch in place. About 1/4" above sleeve bottom, sew two rows of tiny running stitches and pull to gather slightly (opening must fit over doll's hand).

9. As indicated on pattern, sew three rows of gathering stitches on upper bodice both at center front and on back right side. Also, sew three rows of gathering stitches across and above bottom of skirt. Pull and gather top center until top of bodice between sleeve seams is 2" wide. Gather skirt bottom until approximately 4-1/16" wide. Gather top back until approximately 1" wide. Secure all gathering stitches firmly in place.

10. Handstitch neckline hem in place. Then place lace along inside of neckline so that about 1/16" extends above neckline edge. Handstitch in place.

11. From slightly stiffened gauze, cut rectangle 3/4" wide x 13-1/4" long. Turn under bottom hem of gauze strip; press. Sew narrow lace at hemline of gauze strip. Form very narrow knife pleats along its entire length; press. Then stitch in place along raw top edge. Handstitch pleated gauze strip to wrong side of skirt so that approximately 1/8" of lace shows below skirt hem and the raw edge of the pleated gauze strip lines up along top of skirt's gathering stitches.

12. Sew two hooks and eyes at center-back opening.

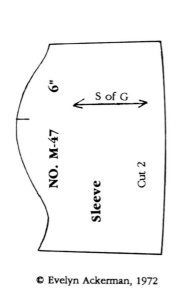

NO. M-47   6"

S of G

Sleeve

Cut 2

© Evelyn Ackerman, 1972

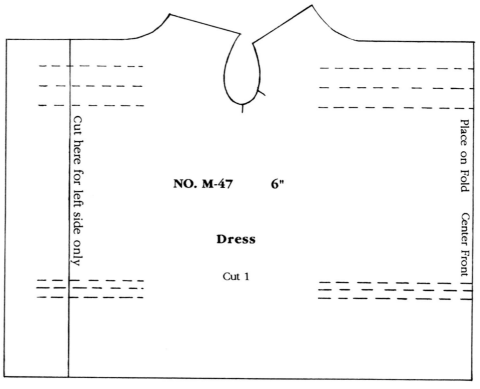

Cut here for left side only

NO. M-47   6"

Dress

Cut 1

Place on Fold   Center Front

PATTERN NO. M-49
FOR A 5 INCH GIRL DOLL'S DRESS

General Instructions

• All pattern parts include 1/8" seams and hems, unless otherwise noted.

• Press all seams and hems as work proceeds.

• Any fabric that is lightweight, pliable and made from a natural fiber can be used. Narrow lace is also required.

Dress

1. Turn under bottom hem. Handstitch in place.

2. Turn under hems of center-back opening. Handstitch in place.

3. Form box pleats at center front and center back as per pattern. Press and baste.

4. To make pleated inserts, cut rectangle 1-5/8" wide x 4-1/2" long for left opening; cut rectangle 1-5/8" wide x 5" long for right opening. Turn under each bottom hem and handstitch in place. Turn under all side seams and press. Place each rectangle next to side of box pleats, matching bottom hemlines and overlapping 1/8" top-seam openings. Slipstitch each side in place. Form three small box pleats to fit opening of each rectangle. Baste and press. Topstitch in place across top of openings.

5. Place flat, narrow lace or other suitable trim across top of pleated inserts, extending under center-front and center-back box pleats. Handstitch in place.

6. Topstitch box pleats in place from raw neckline to top of pleated inserts.

7. With right sides together, sew shoulder seams.

8. Turn under bottom hems of each sleeve. Press and sew in place. With right sides together, sew each sleeve underarm seam.

9. With wrong side of bodice facing you and the sleeve turned to the right side, put the sleeve into the armhole, matching top center to shoulder seam and underarm seam to side seam. Pin in place, easing in cap for smooth fit (use fingers). (To hold sleeve in place where armhole opening is too small for fingers, insert pencil through sleeve opening to hold it in place.) Handstitch sleeve in place. Trim seam. Repeat for other sleeve.

10. Turn under neckline hem and press. Handstitch flat lace or other trim to neckline opening.

11. Sew hooks and eyes to center-back opening. Sew beads or French knots (for simulated buttons) on top center-front and top center-back box pleats (see dots on pattern.)

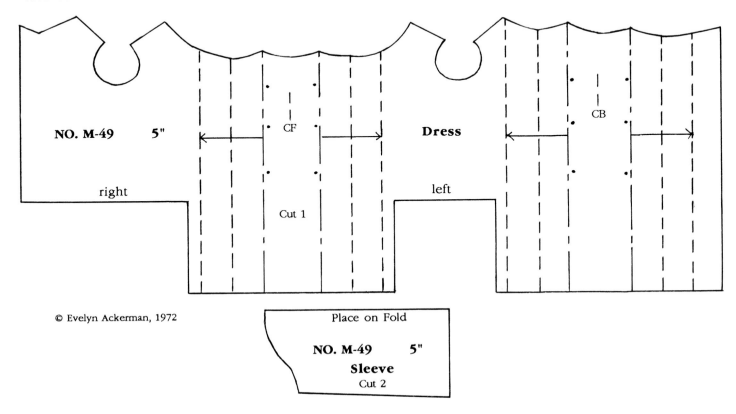

NO. M-49   5"

right

CF

Dress

CB

left

Cut 1

Place on Fold

NO. M-49   5"
Sleeve
Cut 2

PATTERN NO. DH-54
FOR A 5 INCH LADY DOLL'S DRESS

General Instructions

- All pattern parts include very narrow seams and hems, unless otherwise noted.
- Any lightweight fabric made from natural fibers is suitable, especially cotton and silk. Net is required for the bodice (or, if not available, substitute a fine lawn or voile). Very small lengths of lace, both straight-edged and scalloped on one side, are needed.
- Beads are used for decoration.
- Dress is sewn on doll and not removable.

Bodice

1. Pin net under blouse in position on doll in order to hold in place. Overlap center-back opening, turning one side under to form seam, and handstitch in place. Fold narrow, straight-edged lace in half (or use lace net folded with raw edges enclosed), forming neckband. Place at neckline, covering raw edges of bodice neckline and sew at center back.
2. Tack scrap of scalloped lace to center front on chest and straight-edged lace to center back (both approximately two-thirds above bottom of shoulderplate).

3. Bodice over blouse has no pattern, as it is made from scraps and shaping it requires experimentation by pinning it in place after finger manipulation. Cut two dress fabric rectangles 1-1/4" x 2" and two additional ones 1-5/8" x 2" (on front one larger piece overlays the smaller one and this is repeated on the back). These are folded on a diagonal with the point placed at the shoulder. The right side piece overlaps the left side one. Shaping with fingers and needle, with raw edges turned under at shoulders and underarms, sew shoulder and underarm seams, as per drawing.
4. Sew three glass beads at the front and three at the back: place one at the junction of the V neckline and one each at junction of overlay and decorative lace scrap. The beads assist in holding the bodice over blouse in place.
5. For sleeves, cut two net rectangles 1-1/2" x 3". Turn under top and bottom hems. Sew tiny running stitches to top and bottom. Gather sleeve top to fit armhole opening, allowing for underarm seam. Sew in place, overlapping underarm seam and handstitching in place. Gather sleeve bottom to fit arm

and secure in place. Attach narrow, straight-edged lace (same used for neckband) to sleeve bottom to form sleeve band. Gather scalloped lace to fit around sleeve top, at shoulder, forming ruffle. Sew in place. Repeat for other sleeve.

Skirt

1. With right sides together, sew skirt to skirt lining at bottom edge. Trim, turn and press so that lining does not show on right side.
2. Form knife pleats, pinning, pressing and basting in place.
3. Attach five glass beads (to hold pleats in place along each pleat as per dots on pattern).
4. Pin to doll body, with center front at center front of doll. Form tuck pleats at top back, thus pulling rectangle into snug position against body and aligning waist and bottom hem. Tack tuck pleats in place.
5. Overlap one side of center-back opening over other, turning under seam and handstitching in place.
6. Fold fabric rectangle to make cummerbund for waist, turning under raw edges. Sew at center back. Attach ribbon bow-tie at center-back waist.

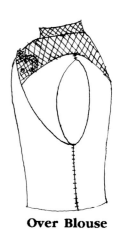

Over Blouse

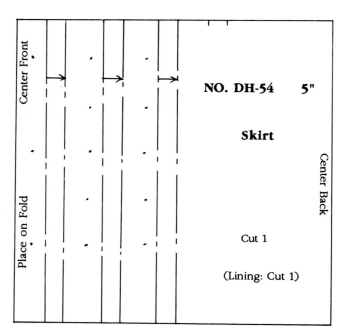

Center Front

Place on Fold

NO. DH-54   5"

Skirt

Center Back

Cut 1

(Lining: Cut 1)

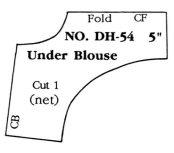

Fold   CF

NO. DH-54   5"

Under Blouse

Cut 1
(net)

CB

126

PATTERN NO. DH-57
FOR A 3-1/2 INCH BOY DOLL'S SUIT

General Instructions

• All pattern parts include very narrow seams and hems, unless otherwise noted.

• Press all seams and hems as work proceeds.

• Any lightweight velvet, wool, or cotton is suitable. For collar and cuffs, use contrasting color and fabric, preferably white cotton (piqué). Very narrow tape is used as trim. Very narrow ribbon tie is placed on jacket.

• Suit is sewn to doll and not removable.

Pants

1. Cut two rectangles of fabric 1-3/4" wide x 1-5/8" high. Turn under bottom hems and sew in place.

2. With right sides together, sew leg seam on each tube from bottom 1/2" up side.

3. Put each leg tube on doll. Sew center-front seam by hand. Tack together at top of center-back opening (it may be necessary to leave remainder of center-back seam open so doll can sit). Pull up as high as possible and then tack tuck pleats in place so pants fit snugly.

Bodice Jacket

1. Slash from neck to bottom only for center-back opening. At front only, deepen V neckline cut, as per dotted line.

2. With right sides together, sew side/arm seams. Clip underarm curves. Turn under bottom hems and sew in place. Sew four or six glass beads to front, double-breasted style.

3. Fit to doll (sleeves may require shortening). With jacket on doll, handstitch center-back opening closed.

4. Cut two cuff rectangles, 5/8" wide x 1-1/8" long. Turn under hems along both lengths and press in place. Fit to doll's wrist (covering sleeve bottom) and sew at side seams.

5. Bend under tiny hems on collar, along all edges. Handstitch narrow tape or braid to front edge (double row, if possible). Place collar around doll's neck, matching center backs. Tack in place. Tack ribbon securely to center front of collar.

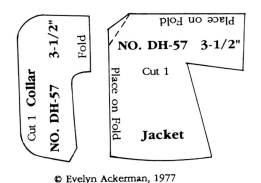

PATTERN NO. DH-58
FOR A 3-1/2 INCH GIRL DOLL'S DRESS

General Instructions

• All pattern parts include very narrow seams and hems, unless otherwise noted.

• Any lightweight fabric made from natural fibers is suitable, especially a colored cotton with a tiny pattern for the skirt and sleeves and a white cotton for the bodice and bertha. One small length of lace is required.

• Dress is sewn to doll and not removable.

Skirt

1. Cut fabric rectangle approximately 1-3/4" wide x 10" long. Repeat for lining. With right sides together, sew skirt to skirt lining along entire bottom edge. Turn and press.

2. Form approximately twelve 1/4" knife pleats. Pin; baste; press.

3. Place around doll's waist. Adjust to fit. Overlap one side of center-back opening over other, turn under seam and sew in place.

Bodice

1. Cut two fabric rectangles (contrast with skirt), 1" wide x 1-3/4" long. Turn under top and bottom hems of each rectangle, lengthwise (one for front of bodice and one for back). Press. (Finished height: 3/4".) Cut each at a diagonal from bottom to top (at sides) so bottom is approximately 1-3/4" wide and top is 3/4" wide. Attach to skirt at waist, overlapping under the arms and tacking firmly in place. Then tack in place at shoulders.

2. For sleeves, cut two rectangles (same fabric as skirt), 1-3/4" wide x 1-1/8" high. Turn under top and bottom hems. Press. Sew tiny running stitches top and bottom. Gather top to fit armhole opening and sew in place, allowing for underarm seam. Sew underarm seam. Gather sleeve bottom to

fit doll's arm. Secure in place.

3. For bertha, cut rectangle (bodice fabric) 3/4" wide x 6" long. Turn under hems along both lengths. Add lace to bottom length. Sew tiny running stitches along top length. Gather to fit

bodice, handstitching in place from back waist alongside sleeve at back, across top of sleeve, down alongside sleeve at front, across bodice front, up alongside sleeve at front, across top of sleeve, down alongside sleeve at back.

PATTERN NO. DH-59
FOR A 6-3/4 INCH GENTLEMAN DOLL'S EVENING SUIT

General Instructions

• All pattern parts include very narrow seams and hems, unless otherwise noted.

• Press all seams and hems as work proceeds.

• The pants, jacket and vest are made from thin black felt. The shirt is made from white cotton. A scrap of narrow ribbon is needed for bow-tie.

• The pants, vest and shirt are made so that they are not removable. It is also best if the jacket is tacked to the doll's cloth body.

Pants

1. With right sides together, sew inside seam of each pant leg. Clip curves.

2. With right sides together, sew center-front seams of legs. Turn. Put on doll and bend under center-back seam as much as necessary. Tuck pleat at each side of waistline and tack tucks in place. Tack center-back seam in place.

Shirt and Vest

1. Fold center-front pleat of shirt. Press. Glue two tiny paper buttons (circles) to center front.

2. Cut narrow rectangle of fabric for neckband (also can substitute narrow white tape or selvage edge of shirt cotton). Tack in place at center front. Add ribbon bow-tie, tacking in place at center front of neckband.

3. Place vest over shirt and tack securely in place. Glue two black paper buttons (circles) to center front.

Jacket

1. With right sides together, sew back to front from armhole opening to dot.

2. Fold center-back pleat so that lower section of jacket back will fit upper section of jacket back, overlapping top section over pleated lower section. Handstitch in place. Press and tack pleats in place.

3. With right sides together, sew shoulder seams.

4. With right sides together, sew sleeve underarm seam. With wrong side of jacket facing you and the sleeve turned to the right side, matching underarm seam to side seam, place sleeve in armhole and handstitch it in place for smooth fit. Hold sleeve securely in place by inserting the index finger in the sleeve opening while sewing (a round pencil may also be helpful). Repeat for other sleeve.

5. The pattern shows the shape of collar/lapel, but it is actually easier to cut a narrow rectangle of felt the proper length to fit around neckline and both sides of jacket front and then shape it to fit neckline. Glue collar/lapel in place. Then glue black glossy paper buttons in place, placing two on each side of center front and two at top of back pleat adjacent to the seams.

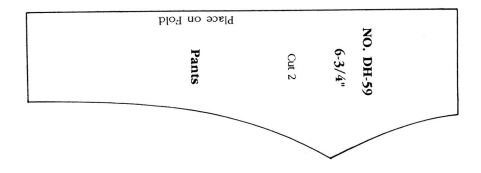

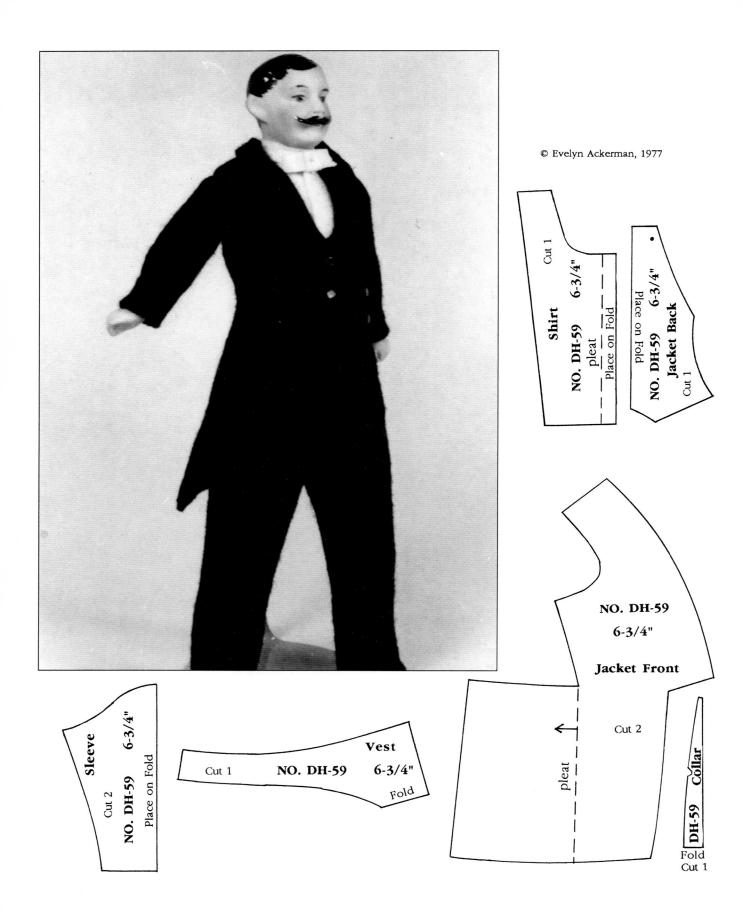

© Evelyn Ackerman, 1977

Shirt Cut 1
NO. DH-59 6-3/4"
pleat
Place on Fold

Place on Fold
NO. DH-59 6-3/4"
Jacket Back Cut 1

NO. DH-59
6-3/4"
Jacket Front
Cut 2
pleat

Sleeve
Cut 2
NO. DH-59 6-3/4"
Place on Fold

Vest
Cut 1 NO. DH-59 6-3/4"
Fold

DH-59 **Collar**
Fold
Cut 1

130

PATTERN NO. DH-62
FOR A 6 INCH LADY DOLL'S DRESS

General Instructions

• All pattern parts include very narrow seams and hems, unless otherwise noted.

• Press all seams and hems as work proceeds.

• Because many dollhouse dolls were made during the first years of the twentieth century, I designed this outfit to fit a 6" high, glass-eyed Simon & Halbig dollhouse doll, an appealing type of miniature doll made for many years. However, any of the Gibson Girl dollhouse dolls, with their high-piled hairdos, also could wear this outfit, inasmuch as they, too, were made during the era when Edwardian fashions—garments characterized by an emphasis on a slender, vertical design—were in vogue.

• Altering the appearance of the garment is easily done in several ways. Two of the simplest means are to use solid, but contrasting colors or solid colors and patterns, together. The kind of fabric and trim materials used can also change the overall effect achieved. If the over blouse is eliminated so that the under blouse becomes the only bodice for the garment, this, too, will make a difference in the final result.

• When following the pattern as shown, the blouse should be made from either a net or a very fine cotton fabric, while the dress can be made from any one of a variety of fabrics, including a closely woven cotton or a lightweight silk. The small size of dollhouse dolls dictates care when selecting fabrics with printed patterns or woven textures, as their scale should relate to the size of the doll. Synthetics, which did not exist before World War I, should be avoided.

• The dress is not removable.

Blouse

1. Slit the center back from top to middle (do not slit the front). With right sides together, sew underarm/side seams. Clip curves.
2. Turn under the narrowest possible (or rolled) hem at the neckline and handstitch in place.
3. Fit the blouse to your doll, overlapping the center-back opening; handstitch in place while on the doll.
4. Using narrow, stiff tape (or other suitable fabric—perhaps the selvage edge of a matching piece of fabric), cover the raw edges of the sleeve bottoms. Handstitch in place.

Bodice Overlay

1. With right sides together, sew the center-front seam.
2. Turn under the hem for the sleeve bottoms and topstitch in place.
3. Turn under the hem for the neckline and topstitch in place.
4. With right sides together, sew the underarm/side seams. Clip curves.
5. Turn under the entire bodice bottom hem; topstitch in place.
6. Sew tiny glass beads (approximately 1/4" apart) to the front of the bottom hem and the entire length of the neckline.
7. Put the overlay on your doll, overlapping the center-back opening for proper fit. Handstitch it in place while on the doll.

Skirt

1. Form the three knife pleats for both skirt bottom inserts. Press the pleats and baste them in place.
2. Turn under the bottom and top hems of both under-strap inserts; baste in place. Overlap each one on top of the "x" side of a pleated insert; baste in place. Turn under all raw edges (except the straight vertical end) of both top-strap inserts; baste in place. Overlap each one on top of the "y" side of a pleated insert and on top of the under-strap inserts; baste in place. Overlap the bottom of both side panels with the top edge of both strap inserts; baste in place. Then topstitch along the top, bottom and points of the strap inserts.
3. Turn under the side seams of the front panel; baste in place. Overlap a side panel (along the dotted line of the "x" side of the bottom insert) with the entire length of the front panel; baste in place. Repeat for other side panel. Topstitch both basted edges.
4. Turn under the side seams of the back panel; baste in place. Overlap a side panel (along dotted line of the "y" side of the bottom insert) on top of the entire length of the back panel, right side only; baste in place. Topstitch both the open and the overlapped side of the back panel.(Remove basted stitches on pleating.)
5. Turn under the hems along all raw edges of the waistline belt (except for the short, straight side); baste in place. Topstitch all edges.
6. Sew tiny glass beads onto the skirt as follows: one at the point of the waistline belt and three along the points of the top-strap inserts.
7. Turn under the bottom hem of the skirt; topstitch in place.
8. Fit the skirt to your doll, overlapping the topstitched left edge of the back panel with the side panel (along the dotted line of the "y" side of the bottom insert); baste in place. Close with tiny overcast stitches.
9. Fit the waistline belt over the top raw edge of the skirt, placing the pointed end over the flat end and centering it so that the glass bead is in the center front. Handstitch in place.

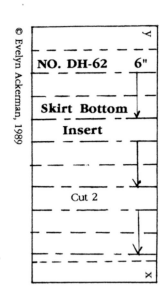

© Evelyn Ackerman, 1989

NO. DH-62   6"

Skirt Bottom
Insert

Cut 2

y

x

DH-62
6"
Cut 2

Top-Strap
Insert

Place on Fold

NO. DH-62   6"

Front and
Back Bodice Overlay

cut on dotted line
for Front Side

Cut 2

Center Front

Center Back

Place on Fold

Blouse Front and Back

underarm

6"

NO. DH-62

Cut 1

Place on Fold

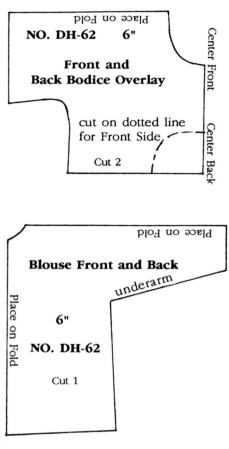

Cut 1   NO. DH-62   6"
Waistline Belt

Place on Fold

NO. DH-62   6"   **Front and Back Skirt Panel**

Cut 2

Skirt Side Panel
NO. DH-62   6"

Place on Fold

Cut 2

DH-62
6"
Cut 2

Under-Strap
Insert

ABOUT THE AUTHOR

Evelyn Ackerman at the time she first began creating patterns for dressing antique dolls.

After obtaining a masters degree in Fine Arts from Wayne University, Detroit, Michigan, Evelyn Ackerman launched her art career, utilizing her skills as designer, craftsman and artist. After many years in which she devoted full time to these endeavors, she joined the research team in the Department of Costume and Textiles at the Los Angeles County Museum of Art where she contributed to the production of several noted exhibitions. She is a charter member of Angels Attic, a toy museum in Santa Monica, California, founded to aid autistic children, where she assists in the research required for acquisitions and exhibitions.

Her articles have been published in prominent collector magazines: *Collectors' Showcase, Dollmaking, Doll News, Doll Reader, Dolls, Inside Collector, International Dolls' House News, Miniature Collector* and *Teddy Bear and Friends.* Evelyn's other published works include *Schoenhut's Humpty Dumpty Circus from A to Z* (in collaboration with Fredrick E. Keller) and two Humpty Dumpty Circus price guides, *Victorian Architectural Splendor in a Nineteenth Century Toy Catalogue, Dolls in Miniature,* and a Los Angeles County Museum of Art catalogue essay, "Dressed for the Country: 1860-1900."